THE IMPORTANCE OF THE
ELECTORAL
COLLEGE

THE IMPORTANCE OF THE ELECTORAL COLLEGE

Dr. George Grant

VISION FORUM MINISTRIES
San Antonio, Texas

"Where there is no vision, the people perish."

Vision Forum Ministries
4719 Blanco Rd., San Antonio, Texas 78212
www.visionforum.org

ISBN 0-9755264-2-1

Cover Design by Shannon G. Moeller
Typesetting by Joshua R. Goforth

PRINTED IN THE UNITED STATES OF AMERICA

Table of Contents

Introduction

The Electoral College is likely to play an ever more significant part in determining the governance of our Republic. The U.S. Constitution spells out the responsibilities of the Legislative Branch in Article I, the Executive Branch in Article II, and the Judicial Branch in Article III.

The Founding Fathers conceived the Electoral College as the best means of choosing a President who would be, at one and the same time, independent of, yet accountable to, the Legislative Branch as well as to the States which voluntarily came together to create our Federal Union, whose delegated, enumerated functions are set forth in the Constitution, with other powers reserved to the States and the people respectively.

The American Republic was founded on the presupposition that we are endowed by our Creator "with certain inalienable rights", that civil "government derives its just powers from the consent of the governed", and that the principal policy-setting institution would be a Congress, consisting of a House chosen by the people, and a Senate, with two members representing each of the States.

Article I, Section One of the Constitution makes clear that "All legislative Powers herein granted shall be vested in a Congress of the United States, which shall consist of a Senate and House of Representatives."

The Federal Republic was to be accountable to the States and the people, with all citizens accountable to their Creator. It was recognized that law is the will of the Sovereign and that God is the ultimate Sovereign authority.

The architecture of the Electoral College established a procedure wherein the Republic's Chief Executive would be chosen by the people as citizens of the States in which they reside.

Instead of a single "national" election, there is a separate election in each of the States which constitute the Republic. In this manner, the President is not the creature of Congress, but an independent force, albeit with actual elements of accountability to the Congress as well as to the States. Moreover, through the Electoral College process, the President is also accountable to "We, the People" as citizens of each particular State.

Because of the Electoral College system, if fraud is detected in a single State's election, it does not de-legitimate or poison the total result. Similarly, the role of the States in choosing the President assures that those who seek the office of chief magistrate will, to a greater degree than would otherwise be the case, pay heed to the varying interests and concerns of the several States.

It is important to note that Electors are chosen in each State in such manner as that State's Legislature may determine. Nowhere in the Constitution is popular election of the President mandated. In times of crisis, be they the result of war, "natural" catastrophe, or acts of terrorism, this fact makes it possible to assure continuity of government even if the "democratic" procedures to which we are accustomed become impractical.

Nowhere in the Constitution is it required that a person chosen to serve as Elector exercise anything but his own independent conscience and reasoning in determining for whom his Electoral vote shall be cast. Although penalties may be applied to "unfaithful" Electors, an Elector may vote for whomever he chooses. Indeed, if, following a popular election prior to the meeting of the Electors in their State capitols, the popular vote winner should die or become incapacitated, this free choice by the Electors can be an extremely important factor.

I encourage you to review the questions and answers which follow this introduction to whet your appetite to learn more about the Electoral College. Later in the report is a complete list of those sections of the Constitution which in some way pertain to the Electoral College and its unique role in American governance.

Howard Phillips

President
The Conservative Caucus Foundation
January 2004

Questions and Answers

1. **Q.** How many electors are in the Electoral College?

    A. There are 538 electors, three for the District of Columbia (in accordance with the 23rd Amendment to the Constitution), two for each of the 50 states (reflecting their equal representation in the U.S. Senate), with the remaining 435 assigned to each state in accordance with the number of its representatives in Congress.

2. **Q.** List two or more 20th century Presidents who were elected without a majority of the popular vote.

    A. In 1912, Woodrow Wilson received 41.8% of the popular vote. In 1916, Woodrow Wilson received 49.3%. In 1948, Harry S. Truman received 49.5%. In 1960, John F. Kennedy received 49.7%. In 1968, Richard M. Nixon received 43.4%. In 1992, William J. Clinton received 43%. In 1996, William J. Clinton received 49%, and, in 2000, George W. Bush received 47.8% of the popular vote.

3. **Q.** List two U.S. Presidents who were elected without a majority in the Electoral College.

    A. In 1800, Thomas Jefferson and his presumed running mate (Aaron Burr) each received 73 votes in the Electoral College. John Adams received 65, Charles Pinckney, 64, and John Jay 1. Because of the tie, the election went to the House of Representatives where, having secured the support of a majority of the states, Jefferson became President. John Quincy Adams in 1824 received 84 electoral votes, compared to 99 for Andrew Jackson, 41 for William H. Crawford, and 37 for Henry Clay. Adams was elected by the House of Representatives with a majority of the state delegations after he struck a deal with Henry Clay.

4. **Q.** What is the name of the only U.S. President who did not receive even a single vote in the Electoral College?

    A. Gerald Ford.

5. **Q.** Who determines how our state's Presidential electors are chosen?

    A. Article II, Section 1 of the Constitution provides that "Each State shall appoint, in such Manner as the Legislature thereof may direct, a Number of Electors, equal to the whole Number of Senators and Representatives to which the State may be entitled in the Congress."

6. **Q.** What are the qualifications to be an elector?

A. The same Article II, Section 1 provision makes clear that "no Senator or Representative, or Person holding an Office of Trust or Profit under the United States, shall be appointed an Elector".

7. Q. Who chooses our state's members of the Electoral College?

A. Currently, all state legislatures have authorized the selection of electors by popular vote.

8. Q. On what date are Presidents elected?

A. The Congress may determine the time of choosing the electors and the day in which they shall give their votes, which day shall be the same throughout the United States, in accordance with Article II, Section 1. Under present law, the electors meet in their state capitals on the first Monday after the second Wednesday in December.

9. Q. On what date are Presidential election results discovered and announced?

A. The votes of the electors certified by the states are sent to Congress, where the President of the Senate opens the certificates and has them counted in the presence of both Houses on January 6, unless January 6 falls on a Sunday, in which case the discovery of the result occurs on January 7.

10. Q. What happens if the leading Presidential candidate dies before the Electoral College meets?

A. The electors may vote for any constitutionally qualified candidate.

11. Q. What happens if the Presidential candidate dies between the date on which the electors meet and the date on which the results of the electors voting becomes public?

A. The Vice President chosen by the electors becomes President-elect.

12. Q. What happens if President Bush and Vice President Cheney are re-elected in 2004 but die before inaugural day on January 20, 2005?

A. According to current laws of succession, the Speaker of the House succeeds to the Presidency.

13. Q. What provisions of the Constitution are particularly relevant to the selection of the President and Vice President?

A. Article II, 12th Amendment, 14th Amendment, 15th Amendment, 19th Amendment, 20th Amendment, 22nd Amendment, 23rd Amendment, 24th Amendment, 25th Amendment, and 26th Amendment.

14. Q. Why did John Wilkes Booth try to assassinate Secretary of State William Seward, as well as President Abraham Lincoln and Vice President Andrew Johnson in April, 1865?

A. To eliminate the President's successor and the official designated by law to call upon the state legislatures to reconstitute their electors.

CHAPTER I

Constitution of the United States

ARTICLE II.

SECTION I.

The executive Power shall be vested in a President of the United States of America. He shall hold his Office during the Term of four Years, and, together with the Vice President, chosen for the same Term, be elected, as follows

Each State shall appoint, in such Manner as the Legislature thereof may direct, a Number of Electors, equal to the whole Number of Senators and Representatives to which the State may be entitled in the Congress: but no Senator or Representative, or Person holding an Office of Trust or Profit under the United States, shall be appointed an Elector.

[The Electors shall meet in their respective States, and vote by Ballot for two Persons, of whom one at least shall not be an Inhabitant of the same State with themselves. And they shall make a List of all the Persons voted for, and of the Number of Votes for each; which List they shall sign and certify, and transmit sealed to the Seat of the Government of the United States, directed to the President of the Senate. The President of the Senate shall in the Presence of the Senate and House of Representatives, open all the Certificates, and the Votes shall then be counted. The Person having the greatest Number of Votes shall be the President, if such Number be a Majority of the whole Number of Electors appointed; and if there be more than one who have such Majority, and have an equal Number of Votes, then the House of Representatives shall immediately chuse by Ballot one of them for President; and if no Person have a Majority, then from the five highest on the List the said House shall in like Manner chuse the President. But in chusing the President, the Votes shall be taken by States, the Representation from each State having one Vote; A quorum for this Purpose shall consist of a Member or Members from two thirds of the States, and a Majority of all the States shall be necessary to a Choice. In every Case, after the Choice of the President, the Person having the greatest Number of Votes of the Electors shall be the Vice President. But if there should remain two or more who have equal Votes, the Senate shall chuse from them by Ballot the Vice President.] [Changed by the Twelfth Amendment.]

The Congress may determine the Time of chusing the Electors, and the Day on which they shall give their Votes; which Day shall be the same throughout the United States.

AMENDMENT XII.

The Electors shall meet in their respective states, and vote by ballot for President and Vice President, one of whom, at least, shall not be an inhabitant of the same state with themselves; they shall name in their ballots the person voted for as President, and in distinct ballots the person voted for as Vice-President, and they shall make distinct lists of all persons voted for as President, and of all persons voted for as Vice-President, and of the number of votes for each, which lists they shall sign and certify, and transmit sealed to the seat of the government of the United States, directed to the President of the Senate; —The President of the Senate shall, in the presence of the Senate and House of Representatives, open all the certificates and the votes shall then be counted; —The person having the greatest number of votes for President, shall be and if no person have such majority, then from the persons having the highest numbers not exceeding three on the list of those voted for as President, the House of Representatives shall choose immediately, by ballot, the President. But in choosing the President, the votes shall be taken by states, the representation from each state having one vote; a quorum for this purpose shall consist of a member or members from two-thirds of the states, and a majority of all the states shall be necessary to a choice. [And if the House of Representatives shall not choose a President whenever the right of choice shall devolve upon them, before the fourth day of March next following, then the Vice-President shall act as President, as in the case of the death or other constitutional disability of the President—] [Superseded by section 3 of the Twentieth Amendment.] The person having the greatest number of votes as Vice-President, shall be the Vice-President, if such number be a majority of the whole number of Electors appointed, and if no person have a majority, then from the two highest numbers on the list, the Senate shall choose the Vice-President; a quorum for the purpose shall consist of two-thirds of the whole number of Senators, and a majority of the whole number shall be necessary to a choice. But no person constitutionally ineligible to the office of President shall be eligible to that of Vice-President of the United States.

Amendment XX.

Section 1.

The terms of the President and Vice President shall end at noon on the 20th day of January, and the terms of Senators and Representatives at noon on the 3rd day of January, of the years in which such terms would have ended if this article had not been ratified; and the terms of their successors shall then begin.

Section 3.

If, at the time fixed for the beginning of the term of the President, the President elect shall have died, the Vice President elect shall become President. If a President shall not have been chosen before the time fixed for the beginning of his term, or if the President elect shall have failed to qualify, then the Vice President elect shall act as President until a President shall have qualified; and the Congress may by law provide for the case wherein neither a President elect nor a Vice president elect shall have qualified, declaring who shall then act as President, or the manner in which one who is to act shall be selected, and such person shall act accordingly until a President or Vice president shall have qualified.

Section 4.

The Congress may by law provide for the case of the death of any of the persons from whom the House of Representatives may choose a President whenever the right of choice shall have devolved upon them, and for the case of the death of any of the persons from whom the Senate may choose a Vice President whenever the right of choice shall have devolved upon them.

CHAPTER 2

The Genius of the Constitutional System

*"The principles of the Constitution form the
bright constellation which has gone before us and
guided our steps through an age of revolution and
reformation. The wisdom of our sages and the blood
of our heroes have been devoted to their attainment.
They should be the creed of our political faith, the
text of civic instruction, the touchstone by which
to try the services of those we trust; and should we
wander from them in moments of error or of alarm,
let us hasten to retrace our steps and to regain the
road which alone leads to peace, liberty, and safety."*

THOMAS JEFFERSON[1]

The English pundit G.K. Chesterton once quipped, "America is the only nation in the world that is founded on a creed."[2] Other nations find their identity and cohesion in ethnicity, or geography, or partisan ideology, or cultural tradition. But the United States were founded on certain other principles— ideas about freedom, about human dignity, and about social responsibility. They are objective concepts– as they must be if they are to take the form of a creed—codified in a sovereign standard of law, a constitution.

This wise American peculiarity in the affairs of men and nations profoundly impressed the brilliant French scholar Alexis de Tocqueville during his famous visit to the United States at the beginning of the nineteenth century. He admiringly called it "American exceptionalism."[3] Sir Henry Maine, the renowned British historian simply called it "the evident genius of the American Constitution."

No other instrument of government—ancient or modern— produced firmer stability, offered more freedom, promoted individual prosperity, or conveyed such hope as this one document. Amazingly, during more than two centuries of social, cultural, political, and technological revolution throughout the entire world, this Constitution has endured, fundamentally unchanged.

All the other European social contracts, manifestos, national charters, and constitutions of the eighteenth century have long since been consigned to the dust bin of history. The lofty ambitions ensconced in the constitutions of Latin America drawn up in the halcyon days of their new-found independence have all since vanished. All the nationalist declarations drawn up in the heady days following the First World War are likewise gone. Those constitutions promulgated at the end of the Second World War have hardly fared better. And there is little doubt that the same fate awaits the emerging democracies that have begun dotting the maps of Europe, Asia, and Africa following the collapse of Communism.

Through it all, the American Constitution has flourished. It is a creed that has withstood every test.

Drawing on a great wealth of sage knowledge and practical experience, the Founding Fathers of the United States codified in their national charter a host of carefully wrought provisions designed to preserve the freedoms and liberties of the people. They designed the government with a series of interlocking checks and balances—not only were the executive, legislative, and judicial branches given spheres of authority over which the others could not interfere, localities, regions, states, and even individuals were afforded certain hedges against the imposition of tyranny. Powers were carefully separated. Authorities were circumspectly delineated. Rights were vigilantly secured.

Rather than yield to the inherent weaknesses of pure democracy, absolute monarchy, elitist oligarchy, radical republicanism, or haughty aristocracy, the Founders created the Constitution as a bastion of mixed government known as Federalism. It was to be a confederation of accountable spheres of authority and covenantal sovereignties. It provided the nation with a government of laws, not rulers. It established a legacy of limited government, as Jefferson asserted, "laced up straitly within enumerated powers."[4]

History has proven the brilliance of the plan. Hardly the fruit of an antiquarian system meant only for an agrarian people, the Constitution's genius is, as President Calvin Coolidge once asserted, "grounded upon a firm foundation of enduring principles, applicable to any society for any time."[5] It is a creed. It is the very quintessence of American exceptionalism.

CHAPTER 3

The Electoral College Flap

*"Every word of the Constitution ultimately decides
a question between power and liberty."*

JAMES MADISON[6]

The Founding Fathers would, more than likely, be surprised by the current controversy over the Electoral College provisions of the Constitution. Indeed, it was one of the least controversial provisions of the new compact during the divisive debate for ratification. According to Alexander Hamilton writing in the *Federalist Papers*, "The mode of appointment of the Chief Magistrate of the United States is almost the only part of the system, of any consequence, which has escaped without severe censure, or which has received the slightest mark of approbation from its opponents. The most plausible of these, who has appeared in print, has even deigned to admit that the election of the President is pretty well guarded. I venture somewhat further, and hesitate not to affirm, that if the manner of it be not perfect, it is at least excellent. It unites in an eminent degree all the advantages, the union of which was to be wished for."[7]

Although it was evident following the election of 1800 that the system needed to be fine-tuned, once the Twelfth Amendment was passed, the structure of the Electoral College was not a matter of serious debate for more than a century—during which time the nation suffered through the traumas of the fiercely contested elections of 1824, 1876, and 1888, to say nothing of the bitter strife of the War Between the States.

Only after the sudden explosive growth of urban America, the precipitous decline of rural populations, and the shifting political influence brought on by the opening of the West and the restoration of the South that the question of the continued necessity of the Electoral College was seriously raised. The debate hardly merited public notice.

But then the election contest of 2000 thrust the issue before the American people as never before. Vice President Al Gore, the Democratic candidate, actually won a slim plurality of the popular vote. Nevertheless, Governor George Bush, the Republican candidate, secured a slight advantage in the Electoral College—thus winning the Presidency. As a result, outraged calls for the abolition of the Constitutional system of election have become commonplace in both the corridors of power in Washington and in the national media outlets. Concerned that "the will of the people" has somehow been "ignored by an archaic system" that "fails to weigh every vote fairly and equally," these critics have demanded that the College be "scrapped for a more direct election process."[8]

According to one long-time critic of the system, Senator Birch Bayh, "the true sentiments of the voters are distorted by the winner-take-all system."[9] In addition, he argued that "population and voter turnout are not accurately reflected. A candidate receiving a plurality of the popular vote in a state whether the margin is one vote or one million carries all the electoral votes of that state, and thus, in effect the minority is disfranchised at an intermediate stage of the electoral process. The winner-take-all system is largely responsible for the possibility of a candidate's being elected President even though he or she polls fewer popular votes than the opponent. Should a candidate receive a minority of the popular vote nationally but carry a sufficient number of states to ensure a majority of the electoral votes, the candidate would be elected, and the will of the majority would be frustrated through the legal and normal operation of the electoral college."[10]

Rather than voting in a direct popular election, U.S. citizens in each state technically choose between slates of electors that represent each party. Taken together, the winning electors form the Electoral College. There are 538 electors, with each state awarded one elector for each of their Congressional representatives and senators (there are three more electors for the District of Columbia). The electors meet after the November popular election to cast their votes and officially elect the President.

The Framers of the Constitution preferred the electoral system to a direct popular election for several reasons. First of all, Alexander Hamilton asserted, "It was desirable that the sense of the people should operate in the choice of the person to whom so important a trust was to be confided. This end will be answered by committing the right of making it, not to any pre-established body, but to men chosen by the people for the special purpose, and at a particular conjuncture."[11] Secondly, he argued, "It was equally desirable, that the immediate election should be made by men most capable of analyzing the qualities adapted to the station, and acting under circumstances favorable to deliberation, and to a judicious combination of all the reasons and inducements which were proper to govern their choice. A small number of persons, selected by their fellow-citizens from the general mass, will be most likely to possess the information and discernment requisite to such complicated investigations."[12] In addition, requiring a candidate to win a majority in the Electoral College was a way of obtaining a national consensus— as Hamilton said, "it was also peculiarly desirable to afford as little opportunity as possible to tumult and disorder. This evil was not least to be dreaded in the election of a magistrate, who was to have so important an agency in the administration of the government as the President of the United States. But the precautions which have been so happily concerted in the system under consideration, promise an effectual security against this mischief."[13]

Critics of the Electoral College system say its chief fault is that a President can be elected without winning a majority of the popular vote. In fact, a President with a minority of the popular vote has won the Electoral College vote 15 times in U.S. history, most recently in 1992 and 1996, when William Clinton won only 43 percent and 49 percent of the popular vote respectively.

The critics argue that the Electoral College also tends to over-represent voters in rural states. In 1988, the seven least populous jurisdictions (including the District of Columbia) had 21 electoral votes, the same as Florida. But Florida's population was three times the combined population of those seven jurisdictions.

Perhaps more ominously, critics also argue that because the Constitution allows electors to use their discretion, there is a possibility of a "faithless" elector not casting his vote for the people's choice but for his own preference. This has only happened seven times and never had a real effect on the outcome of an election. Electors now are usually pledged to support a party's candidate.

Worst of all, the critics say, each state's electoral votes are awarded on a winner-take-all basis in the Constitutional system. This makes it extremely difficult for third party or independent candidates to win any votes in the Electoral College. State legislatures are free, however, to reject the "winner-take-all" system. In fact, by concentrating support in certain states, a candidate can take the Presidency without winning more popular votes than his opponent. For example, in 1876 Rutherford B. Hayes lost the popular vote by several percentage points but carried the Electoral College, thus winning the election over Samuel Tilden, his Democratic opponent.

Indeed, as the state's representatives were apportioned according to the 1990 census, a presidential candidate only needs to win 11 of the most heavily populated of the 50 states in order to take the Presidency—California, Texas, Florida, New York, Ohio, Pennsylvania, Illinois, Michigan, New Jersey North Carolina, and either Georgia or Virginia. If a candidate wins a slim majority in California and grabs its 54 electoral votes, he is fully one-fifth of the way to the 270 electoral votes needed to capture the Presidency. Thus while California is the nation's most populous state, accounting for 11 percent of the U.S. population, its electoral votes are an even greater prize, 20 percent of the necessary votes.

So what exactly is the value of the Electoral College? How should we answer the critics of the Electoral College provisions of the Constitution? Should the current movement for substantial electoral reform be countenanced at all? The wisdom of the Founding Fathers provides the clues.

CHAPTER 4

Historical Rationale

*"A contempt of the monuments and the wisdom of
the past, may be justly reckoned one of the reigning
follies of these days, to which pride and idleness
have equally contributed...."*

SAMUEL JOHNSON[14]

The essential philosophical and structural framework within which the Founding Fathers constructed their innovative scheme of national checks and balances, separation of powers, and mixed government was state confederation—or federalism.

The principle of federalism allows distinctive and individual communities to join together for a greater good without losing their essential distinctiveness and individuality. Instead of the states becoming a part of some larger amorphous union, under federalism they are able to unite in a symbiotic fashion so that the sum of their parts is greater than that of the whole.

A federal relationship is a kind of compact or covenant that allows states to bind themselves together substantially without entirely subsuming their sundry identities and powers. The federal nature of the American Constitutional covenant enables the nation to function as a republic, thus specifically avoiding the dangers of a pure democracy.

Republics exercise governmental authority through mediating representatives under the rule of law. Pure democracies on the other hand exercise governmental authority through the imposition of the will of the majority without regard for the concerns of any minority—thus allowing law to be subject to the whims, fashions, and fancies of men. The Founders designed the federal system of the United States so that the nation could be, as John Adams described it, a "government of law, not of men."[15]

The Founders thus expressly and explicitly rejected the idea of a pure democracy, because, as James Madison declared, "democracies have ever been spectacles of turbulence and contention; have ever been found incompatible with personal security, or the rights of property; and have in general been as short in their lives, as they have been violent in their deaths." The rule of the majority does not always respect the rule of law, and is as turbulent as the caprices of political correctness. Indeed, history has proven all too often that democracy is particularly susceptible to the urge and impulses of "mobocracy."[16]

Federalism balances the vertical and horizontal aspects of a covenant. Vertically, Americans are one people under the rule of common law. Horizontally though, Americans are differentiated into a number of distinctive communities— sovereign states—protected from the possible intrusions of the national government or from a majority of the other communities.

As educator Paul Jehle has argued, "The nature of federalism is seen in the balanced structure of the states and the people throughout the Constitution. Both the national government and State governments are sovereign in their respective spheres. Our national identity as Americans, and our federal identity as state citizens, are both represented in Congress—in the Senate and House."[17]

The Electoral College was originally designed by the Founding Fathers as a *federal hedge against the domination of the absolute national majority over the individual states*. Without the College, the delicate federal balance between national unity and regional distinctiveness would be lost and the various states would lose much of their power over the Executive Branch.

The Electoral College was thus designed to be a method of indirect but popular election of the President of the United States. The Framers of the Constitution were careful to follow clear principle in this design—it was hardly a matter of haphazardness or convenience. They wanted a federal means to elect the Chief Magistrate of the nation so that careful and calm deliberation would lead to the selection of the best-qualified candidate.

Thus, voters in each state actually cast votes for electors who are pledged to vote for a particular candidate. These electors, in turn, choose the President and Vice-President. The number of electors for each state equals the numerical total of its Congressional representation. After Election Day, on the first Monday after the second Wednesday in December, these electors assemble in their state capitals, cast their ballots, and officially select the next President of the United States. The candidate who receives the most votes in a state at the general election will generally be the candidate for whom the electors later cast their votes. Presently, the candidate who wins in a state is awarded all of that state's Electoral College votes; *Maine and Nebraska are the only exceptions to the winner-take-all rule.* There is no Constitutional requirement regarding apportionment of electoral votes.

The votes of the electors are then sent to Congress where the President of the Senate opens the certificates and counts the votes. This takes place on January 6, unless that date falls on a Sunday. In that case, the votes are counted the next day.

An absolute majority is necessary to prevail in the Presidential and the Vice Presidential elections, that is, half the total plus one electoral vote. Thus, with 538 Electors, a candidate must receive at least 270 votes to be elected to the office of President or Vice President.

Should no Presidential candidate receive an absolute majority, the House of Representatives determines who the next President will be, choosing among the three who have received the greatest number of electoral votes. Each state may cast one vote and an absolute majority is needed to win. Similarly, the Senate, by majority vote of its members, decides whom the next Vice President will be if there is no absolute majority after the Electoral College vote, choosing between the top two candidates.

This federal design ultimately means that the Electoral College is a hedge of protection against several deleterious aspects of pure numerical democracy: There were four good reasons the Framers rejected direct election of the President.

The Framers rejected direct popular election of the President because it failed to protect the states from the intrusion of massed centralized forces. They reasoned that a pure democracy was more easily corrupted than a federal republic. It would essentially eliminate state borders and state prerogatives; whenever more centralized government directly governs the people, they thought that there was likely to be more opportunity for corruption.

Electing the President by the Legislative or Judicial branches would violate the separation of powers. Thus, the federal solution was to elect the President by a balanced representation of the states and the people. Electors were to be elected in accordance with standards established by the State legislatures, and the electors were then to elect the President. This federal approach carefully avoided direct dependency upon either the states or the people, but kept both represented in the process. Giving each State the same number of electors as they have representatives in Congress was also in harmony with this balance.

Direct popular election of the President was rejected by the Framers because it would fail to prevent candidates from pandering to one region, or running up their votes in certain states. Political scientist James Whitson explained the problem with a sports analogy: "In a baseball season you don't play 100 odd games, add up your total runs from all those games, and the teams with the most [runs] play in the World Series. Teams would just run up the score on weaker teams to balance the closer games against tougher opponents. In a direct election, Democrats would run up the vote totals in safe states like Massachusetts and Republicans would run up their votes in states like Nebraska. The Electoral College forces candidates to concede states their opponents are winning handily and contest the tight races."[18]

A third reason direct popular election of the President was rejected by the Framers was that it would fail to protect minority interests from a tyrannical majority. For example in a direct election, since African-Americans account for about 13% of the population, they could only account for 13% of the vote. In the Electoral College, African-Americans account for 25% of Alabama's 9 votes, 27% of Georgia's 13 votes, 31% of Louisiana's 9 votes, etc., thus securing more political power where their gross numbers are greater.

Farmers, once a very influential constituency, now make up less than 4% of the population. Why would a candidate worry about this small group in a direct election? In the Electoral College system, *farmers* do make up sizable parts of several states, and thus their combined strength in a smaller pool of voters gives them more power. Thus we see again that because minority groups are often concentrated in some states and not spread evenly throughout the country, their influence is protected to a greater degree in a federal system.

Finally, the Framers avoided direct democracy because it would fail to prevent candidates from ignoring smaller states in favor of big metropolitan areas. In a direct election, New York City would have about twice the combined electoral clout of Alaska, Delaware, Montana, North Dakota, Vermont, and Wyoming. *Why would a candidate even campaign in those six states when he can double his impact by spending more time and less money in a single city?* The needs and issues of small rural communities would be ignored by the candidates in favor of the more politically powerful urban areas.

The Electoral College system thus represents the careful implementation of an essential Constitutional principle: federalism. Without it, the genius of the whole Constitution would be jeopardized.

CHAPTER 5

The Elections of 1789, 1792, and 1796

"Posterity: you will never know how much it has cost my generation to preserve your freedom. I hope you will make good use of it."

JOHN QUINCY ADAMS[19]

When the the States finally ratified the Constitution and the time arrived for the new federal republic to elect its first President in 1789, there really was only one choice for the Electors of the Electoral College: George Washington. He was a delegate to Congress, commander-in-chief of the Continental Army during the War for Independence, and the unanimously elected President of the Constitutional Convention.

His popularity cut across the political spectrum, including those who advocated a strong central government (the Federalists), those who wanted the states to hold the most power (soon to be known as the Democratic-Republicans), and even those who did not much care about politics at all. From *the 69 electors* who had to name two choices for President on their ballot, Washington received one vote on every ballot—in a sense, a unanimous affirmation. Nevertheless, 11 other men also garnered votes, including three former Presidents of Congress of the earlier American government under the Articles of Confederation.

His first administration was marked by the emergence of partisan bickering between the Federalists and the Democratic-Republicans. President Washington, who had originally hoped to retire after his first term, decided to run again in 1792 to try to unify the country and to discourage the party spirit. The Democratic-Republicans, who were aware of Washington's obvious and undiminished popularity and who were at the time out-manned and out-numbered by the Federalists, did not oppose his reelection. Once again Washington received a vote on every elector's ballot, with five other men also receiving votes.

With the retirement of George Washington, the political parties began their dominating influence over Presidential politics in the election of 1796. In Congress members of each faction met together and would decide whom to support for President. The electors who would choose the President were picked by the states, using various methods, including decisions by state legislatures, and popular election by Congressional district.

The Federalists in Congress met in caucus, throwing their support to Washington's Vice President John Adams for President and Thomas Pinckney, a diplomat from South Carolina, for Vice President. The Democratic-Republican members met and determined to support former Secretary of State Thomas Jefferson for President and Aaron Burr, a Senator from New York, for Vice President.

After eight years of having to keep their opposition to Washington's policies toned down to avoid the appearance of offending the popular President, the Democratic-Republicans vociferously attacked Adams. They accused the Vice President of attempting to resurrect the prerogatives of a monarchy. Adams accused Jefferson of demagoguery—preying on the fears of the people in an attempt to conjure up votes.

Because the Constitution was not written with political parties in mind, this election would be the first of two in a row in which an unexpected situation would develop. At that time, electors voted for two candidates for President; no mention of Vice President was made on the ballot. After all the votes were tallied, the person with the majority of votes was named President and the runner-up was declared Vice President. The political parties, however, did not just run candidates for President. They ran teams of candidates with one man designated specifically for the runner-up spot of Vice President.

Alexander Hamilton, a Federalist who did not want either Adams or Jefferson to win, devised a plan to give the Presidency to Thomas Pinckney, Adams' running mate. Hamilton secretly tried to get southern electors who had planned to vote for both Adams and Pinckney to leave Adams off their ballot. New England electors, not knowing of the scheme, would dutifully cast their ballots for both Adams and Pinckney. The effect would be that Pinckney would receive more votes than Adams and would become President. Hamilton's plan fell apart at the last minute when the New England electors became aware of the scheme and countered it by leaving Pinckney off their ballots.

In the end, Adams received 71 electoral votes and was named President. However, because of Hamilton's botched scheme, Pinckney was omitted from too many ballots and was not the runner-up. Adam's chief opponent, Thomas Jefferson, placed second with 68 electoral votes and became Vice President.

CHAPTER 6

The Election of 1800

*"The Constitution is not an instrument for
government to restrain the people,
it is an instrument for the people to
restrain the government—
lest it come to dominate our
lives and interests."*

PATRICK HENRY[20]

The electoral system was devised by the Founding Fathers as a means to entrust the responsibility of selecting the nation's chief executive to people whose choice would be more or less unaffected by partisan political rancor. In Article II, Section 1, of the Constitution, the method of selecting electors is delegated to the separate state legislatures, and the voting procedure to be followed by the electors is carefully defined. According to the electoral procedure originally defined, the electors were instructed to vote for the two most qualified persons without specifying which was preferred for President and which for Vice President. The candidate receiving the greatest number of electoral votes, provided the votes of a majority of the electors were received, would become the

President, and the candidate winning the second largest number of votes would be Vice President.

A flaw in this procedure was revealed in the election of 1800, when Thomas Jefferson was the Presidential candidate of the Democratic-Republicans and Aaron Burr was the party's candidate for Vice President. The electors, by voting strictly for candidates of their party, gave Burr and Jefferson the same number of votes. As the Constitution provided, the election was then referred to the House of Representatives, where a protracted struggle took place, requiring *thirty-six ballots* before Jefferson was chosen President and Burr Vice President.

After the failed machinations of Alexander Hamilton in the election of 1796 and the unexpected gridlock of the election of 1800, it was clear that the Constitutional provisions for the Electoral College needed adjustment. Thus, one of the first tasks of the new Jefferson administration was to propose the Twelfth Amendment.

CHAPTER 7

The Twelfth Amendment

"Government is but a tool. If ever we come to the place where our tools determine what jobs we can or cannot do, and by what means, then nary a fortnight shall pass in which new freedoms shall be wrested from us straightway. Societal problems are solved by families and communities as they carefully and discriminately use a variety of tools."

HENRY CABOT LODGE

As the Founders originally intended in the Constitution, the election process was to be a contest of individuals, not political parties. With a man like George Washington, whose popularity was virtually universal among the voters, this system worked well enough. But during the two elections that followed, the rise of political factions produced some unexpected outcomes. As a result, the Twelfth Amendment, ratified in 1804, changed the way the Vice President is elected. The amendment simply provided for separate ballot lines for President and Vice President, and reduced from five to three the number of candidates to be considered if the election went to the House of Representatives.

Today when an elector casts his ballot he lists one person as his choice for President and another as his choice for Vice President. Then two separate lists are drawn up, one with all the names and votes cast for President, and another with all the names and votes cast for Vice President. The person with a majority of votes on the Presidential list is named President and the person with a majority of votes on the Vice Presidential list is named Vice President. If no one receives a majority of votes for President, the House of Representatives chooses from the top three candidates. If no one receives a majority of the votes for Vice President, the Senate chooses from the top two candidates. Before 1804, when an elector cast his ballot, he listed his top two choices for President. The choices were not ranked as "first choice" or "second choice" and no mention was made of Vice President. One list was then drawn up that included both names from every elector's ballot. The person with the majority of votes from the total number of electors (not the majority of the total number of electoral votes) was named President. The person with the next highest number of votes became Vice President. If two people had a majority and the same number of votes, then the House of Representatives would choose between them which would be President; the other would be Vice President. If no one received a majority then the House would choose the President from the top five candidates. From the remaining four, the one with the most electoral votes would be Vice President. If two or more people were tied for second on the list the Senate would choose among them the Vice President.

Clearly, the Twelfth Amendment made the possibility of electoral chaos much less likely. Indeed, since its passage, only two elections have been thrown to the House of Representatives—and one of those was due largely to the continuing political effects of the War Between the States and Reconstruction.

CHAPTER 8

The Election of 1824

"We have received the Constitution as the work of the assembled wisdom of the nation. We have trusted to it as to the sheet anchor of our safety in the stormy times of conflict with a foreign or domestic foe. We have looked to it with sacred awe as the palladium of our liberties, and with all the solemnities of religion have pledged to each other our lives and fortunes here and our hopes of happiness hereafter in its defense and support. Were we mistaken, my countrymen, in attaching this importance to the Constitution? No. We were not mistaken. The letter of this great instrument is free from radical fault. No, we did not err."

ANDREW JACKSON[21]

Despite its long-term success and stability, critics of the Electoral College point to the elections of 1824, 1876, 1888, and now 2000 to suggest that the system simply does not work. In each of these elections the candidate who won the Electoral College vote did not win the popular vote. Each of these elections, however, was marked by peculiar circumstances.

For instance, the critics charge that in the election of 1824, Andrew Jackson won both the electoral vote and the popular vote, but the House of Representatives circumvented the will of the people and chose John Quincy Adams as President. In reality, the situation was not quite so straightforward.

In this election five men were running for President. Each was popular in a different section of the country: Adams in the Northeast, Jackson in the Southwest, William Crawford in the Southeast, Henry Clay in the West, and John C. Calhoun in the Mid-Atlantic. When the votes were counted, Jackson had won the most electoral and popular votes, but had failed to carry a majority of electoral votes. It fell to the House of Representatives to choose the President from among the top three electoral vote getters: Jackson, Adams, and Crawford. Clay threw his support to Adams—who was rumored to have offered his former rival a cabinet post in exchange for the support of his constituency. Whether back-room wheeling and dealing took place or not, Adams carried the vote on the first ballot and was named President.

As it turned out, the campaign of 1824 was actually more about the personalities of the candidates and their respective regional rivalries than partisan politics and divisive national issues. John Quincy Adams of Massachusetts, son of former President John Adams, had a very formal and deliberate manner. He had served as a minister to the Netherlands, Prussia, Russia and Britain, as a U.S. Senator, and as President Monroe's Secretary of State. He was the author of the Monroe Doctrine and was the most experienced politician among the distinguished slate of candidates.

Andrew Jackson of Tennessee was considered by many much more down-to-earth and a man of the people, altogether unlike every other President up to that time. He was also an extremely popular war hero and territorial governor. Besides his military experience, he had served in Congress as both a Representative and a Senator, and had spent time as a state judge.

William Crawford of Georgia was the chosen candidate of the last of the Congressional caucuses, party assemblies which had gradually become unpopular with the people, who saw them as aristocratic, elitist, and undemocratic. He had served as a Senator, a minister to France, and Secretary of the Treasury for both the Madison and Monroe Administrations. However, his nomination by the caucus system hurt his chances considerably. In addition, about a year before the election he suffered a paralytic stroke that weakened him physically throughout the campaign.

Henry Clay of Kentucky was a popular legislator who would later earn the nickname "The Great Compromiser." Like Jackson, he was seen as closer to the people than blue-blood aristocrats like Adams and Crawford. He served as a state legislator and in Congress as both a Senator and a Representative. Clay was a formidable candidate and party leader.

John C. Calhoun of South Carolina served as a state legislator, a U.S. Representative, and President Monroe's Secretary of War. Late in the race he dropped out of contention and instead became the Vice Presidential favorite for both Adams and Jackson.

Supporters of each candidate focused less on issues and more on the character traits of their opponents. Political and personal mudslinging became commonplace. Adams was mocked for his careless appearance and formal manners. Jackson was accused of being a brutal butcher of Indians on the frontier– and far too fond of the code duello to be President. Crawford was charged with misconduct in his official duties. Clay was known to be a corrupt politician and an immoral drunkard.

Following the general election, when the votes were finally counted, Jackson led both in the popular vote and the Electoral College. However, he did not have a majority of the electoral votes so, following instructions set out in the Constitution, the House of Representatives chose the President from among the top three electoral vote getters: Jackson, Adams, and Crawford.

Clay was the Speaker of the House and there was much talk of whether he would use his influence as Speaker and as a former candidate to sway the vote. A rumor surfaced that Clay had approached the Adams and Jackson campaigns and offered his support in return for the post of Secretary of State. He flatly denied the charge, and no evidence was ever brought forward to prove it. When the House met to vote, it only took one ballot for them to declare Adams the President.

Jackson's supporters were upset and claimed that the will of the people had been ignored because he had won the popular vote. While technically true, "Jacksonians" ignored the fact that the Hero himself would have been a minority President, having nearly 58% of the popular vote against him. Furthermore, six states did not have a public vote, with the legislature choosing the electors, as they were entitled to do in accordance with Article II, Section One of the U.S. Constitution.

Since Jackson received only 21% of the electoral vote from these six states (compared to 51% for Adams), Adams' popular vote may have suffered by having these states excluded. Nevertheless, the outrage of Jackson's supporters only increased when several days later Adams named Clay his Secretary of State. "Corrupt Bargain" became the cry of protesters who believed their man had been robbed of the Presidency. They would have their revenge four years later.

This was a case where, far from failing, the Electoral College functioned precisely as it was intended. It was in Congress, if anywhere, that the "Corrupt Bargain" was struck—which raises a whole separate set of issues.

CHAPTER 9

The Election of 1876

"The Constitution, our bulwark of liberty, is the closest instrument we have to earthly justice and fairness. Should the apparatus fail to support our particular preferences at the moment, we can yet be assured that it will protect us ultimately, in the long term. Ours is not a compact for a moment, but for perpetuity."

SAMUEL TILDEN[22]

In the election of 1876, critics of the Electoral College assert the system failed because, even though Samuel Tilden had a substantial lead over Rutherford B. Hayes in the popular vote, he still lost by one electoral vote. Again though, the circumstances of this post-war race were hardly normative.

On election night, it indeed appeared that Tilden would win. He led the popular vote 51% to 48%, and led in the Electoral College vote 184-165 with 20 votes still undecided. Tilden only needed one vote to win; Hayes needed all 20. Both parties claimed the disputed votes—Florida's 4 votes, Louisiana's 8 votes, South Carolina's 7 votes, and 1 of Oregon's 3 votes.

Congress established an Electoral Commission which awarded all 20 votes, and the Presidency, to Hayes.

The 1876 election was filled with so many irregularities that blaming the Electoral College for not reflecting the will of the voters seems more than a little disingenuous.

A massive amount of *fraud* was documented in the states of Florida, Louisiana, and South Carolina. Democrats intimidated former slaves in order to keep them from voting, and Republicans, backed by armed troops, transported those former slaves from one polling place to another to vote—as many times as they could manage. It is now difficult to say who would have legitimately won those states, but most scholars agree that Tilden would likely have won Louisiana and Florida, and Hayes would have carried South Carolina.

Finally, the Electoral Commission set up by Congress was not part of the normal Electoral College system. It was composed of 8 Republicans and 7 Democrats who voted to give all the votes to Hayes. The Republicans had secretly made a deal with the Democrats. If the Democrats would accept the results of the Electoral Commission, the Republicans would end Reconstruction in the South and appoint a Democrat as Postmaster General, the most important patronage job in the Federal government.

To claim that the Electoral College failed in 1876 ignores the extraordinary circumstances of the election. Without considering either the rampant fraud in the South or the biased Electoral Commission the popular vote winner, Tilden, probably would have won the electoral vote as well.

CHAPTER 10

The Election of 1888

"The Constitution affords us the best possible protection, in this poor fallen world, against the graft and corruption of our electoral system. It offers us the assurance that while not every right cause will prevail at the moment, yet in the end, the truth will surely out."

GROVER CLEVELAND[23]

In the election of 1888, critics of the federal system believe they have their best case against the Electoral College. Grover Cleveland won the popular vote while Benjamin Harrison won the electoral vote. Since no major issues of fraud, voter irregularities, or Congressional meddling were alleged, this election appears to offer a straightforward case of the system failing to award the office to the winner.

The incumbent Democratic President Cleveland attempted to make the tariff the central issue in the campaign. He proposed that Congress substantially lower controversial import taxes, a move widely favored in the South. The Republican challenger, Harrison, focused on a much wider range of issues—but wanted to keep high tariffs, a policy widely favored in much of the rest of the country.

The campaign proved to be one of the most civil and boring in history. It was also one of the closest. Cleveland won by only 0.8% over Harrison in the popular vote. That lead was concentrated in a single region while Harrison was able to appeal to a broader constituency across the whole nation.

While critics claim this as their best example of how flawed the Electoral College system actually is, supporters argue that on the contrary, this election shows why the system works. The Electoral College system encourages candidates to make their appeal as broad as possible in order to win. Cleveland ran a campaign based on one issue supported by a single region of the country and ran up the vote in that region, thereby padding his popular vote.

In the six southern states of Alabama, Georgia, Louisiana, Mississippi, South Carolina, and Texas, Cleveland received more than 65% of the vote. In those six states Cleveland beat Harrison by 425,532 votes. In the other 32 states combined, Harrison beat Cleveland by 334,936 votes.

To say the Electoral College failed in 1888 is to miss the very genius of the federal philosophy of regional protection. The Electoral College prevents one region of the country voting as a block from unduly directing the outcome of the election. The real reason Cleveland won the popular vote, by a mere 90,536 out of 11,379,131 votes cast, but lost the election, was the unusually high support in a single region of the country.

CHAPTER II

The Election of 2000

Critics of the Electoral College have protested long and loud since the election of 2000—a very bitterly fought and close race, though by no means the most bitter or the closest. Neither candidate, Democratic Vice President Al Gore and Republican Governor George Bush, won as much as 50% of the popular vote—with Gore having a very slight advantage. Bush however was able to eke out a win in the Electoral College after several conflicted and divided court decisions.

Where the results of the 2000 electoral totals are doubtful—because of under-votes, over-votes, faulty ballots, judicial interference, or Byzantine legislative machinations—the fault does not lie with the Electoral College. Indeed, the system proved itself capable of doing precisely what the Founders had intended in the first place.

As was the case in the Cleveland-Harrison election, Gore's appeal was much more limited regionally than was Bush's. In fact, George Bush won 29 states to Gore's 21. Bush won 2,436 counties but Gore received majorities in only 676. Bush won in regions covering approximately 2,432,456 square miles of the nation while Gore won in 575,184. The electoral map indicates a huge mandate for Bush, but because Gore's votes were concentrated in a few urban areas, he was able to run up vote totals that skewed the overall percentages.

Once again, the Electoral College functioned precisely as the Founders had intended by preserving the federal nature of the American republic.

2000 ELECTORAL VOTE

ELECTORAL VOTE
TOTAL: 537
NOT VOTING: 1

Republican (G.W. Bush)
Democratic (Gore)

CHAPTER 12

Arguments for the Retention of the College

*"Towards the preservation of your government and
the permanency of your present happy state, it is
requisite, not only that you steadily discountenance
irregular oppositions to its acknowledged authority,
but also that you resist with care the spirit of
innovation upon its principles, however specious the
pretexts. One method of assault may be to effect,
in the forms of the Constitution, alterations which
will impair the energy of the system, and thus to
undermine what cannot be directly overthrown."*

GEORGE WASHINGTON[24]

The Electoral College system has much to commend it—
not the least of which is the record of more than two
centuries of competent and consistent performance. But its role
in the preservation of the federal system of checks and balances
is perhaps the most compelling argument of all. Very simply,
the Electoral College provides protection for minorities against
the tyranny of the 51%. The vaunted "will of the people" is
not best expressed in the voices of just over half of the people

if just under half of the people have their voices ignored. The brilliance of the Constitutional system is precisely that every vote counts, not just those that belong to the majority.

If the federal hedge of the Electoral College were not in place then it would be perfectly possible for a candidate to lose as many as 49 states and still win the Presidency. Imagine the chaos if George Bush had won every state but lost Massachusetts by a popular vote margin sufficient to cost him the Presidency. If he had won each of those states by fairly small margins—akin, say, to his actual margin of victory in Florida—his lead might amount to less than half a million overall. If Gore had won Massachusetts by a million votes—mostly from the city of Boston and its suburbs—then Gore would have won the overall popular vote total, despite having lost 49 of the 50 states. His popular vote would be 500,000 votes more than Bush's. With the Electoral College, Bush would have won 525-13. In a direct election, Gore would have prevailed. If the best argument that direct election proponents have is that the Electoral College is not fair, it would be altogether legitimate to pose the following question: *Is it fair for a candidate to only get a majority of the votes in one state and still become President of all fifty?*

Consider how population massing can skew the results of a national election. The total combined population of the 15 states of Alaska, Delaware, Hawaii, Idaho, Maine, Montana, Nebraska, Nevada, New Hampshire, New Mexico, North Dakota, Rhode Island, South Dakota, Vermont, and Wyoming is about 16 million. The total combined population of New York, Los Angeles, Chicago, and Houston is about 16 million. The smallest of these states, Rhode Island, encompasses a little under 1500 square miles. The combined area of the four largest American cities is just over 1500 square miles. In a direct election, the people of just four cities would have the equivalent of the electoral clout of the people in 15 states. Thus, in a direct election people in large cities would be given preferential treatment by the candidates because it would be less expensive and more efficient for them to spend their time there.

Curtis Gans, founder and director of the Committee for the Study of the American Electorate, has argued that direct election would likely cause more problems than it would solve. "The idea of getting rid of the Electoral College would be profoundly dangerous, particularly in the present way that we conduct our campaigns," he asserted. "Essentially what this would mean is that the totality of our campaigns would be a television advertising, tarmac kind of campaign. You would be handing the American Presidential campaign to whatever media adviser could out-slick the other.[25]

Gans contended that the case for keeping the indirect approach to electing Presidents represented by the Electoral College, is not nearly so simple and clear as the case for direct elections, but it is, in his view, more persuasive. It rests on four critical concepts: manipulation, grassroots engagement, pluralism, and participation.

First, he declared that the central question in the creation of any system of election is its incentive structure—what activities it encourages and what it does not. "Arguably the worst thing that has happened in the modern era to the conduct of American politics is the coaxial cable and the free rein it has given political consultants to pollute our airwaves with attack

.ads every biennium—driving up the cost of campaigns, driving voters both from the polls and increasingly from respect either of political leadership or the political process as a whole."

While even with the Electoral College, increasingly the bulk of campaign resources are poured into televised political advertising, *direct elections would insure that all monetary resources would be poured into such advertising.* There would be virtually no incentive to try to mobilize constituencies, organize specific interests or devote any resources to such things as voter registration and education. The result of direct elections is that campaigns would be run on the basis of polling the gross number of likely voters across America and targeting television messages to their interests and views. Our election would, in essence, not be a contest between two putative Presidents, but rather between two would-be king-makers—Squiers vs. Sipple—in a race to the bottom to see who can do the better job of turning off the other's potential voters.

"What we would have is a political system that combines the worst of network television with the worst of the modern campaign. Network television, as one may note, devotes three hours every evening to pursuing precisely the same audience with precisely the same unedifying fare of sit-coms, shoot-em-ups, and disaster series aimed, so they believe, at capturing the biggest share of the widest possible audience. Which may, in turn, explain the decline in civic literacy and, more recently, in the age of cable and satellite, the decline in network viewership. Couple that with the unrelentingly demagogic negative tone of the political ad campaign and we have a recipe for not, in my friend

Newt Minow's words, an intellectual wasteland, but a political wasteland of citizens permanently tuned out to politics."[26]

Second, he argued, the same incentives that would, under a direct election system, propel all campaign resources into television advertising would virtually eliminate any resources devoted to grassroots and citizen involvement. "Under the electoral college, there is a strong incentive—at least in some states—for campaigns, interests, and others to organize groups on the grassroots level because some of those groups may be determinative in winning state electoral votes. It is no secret that advocacy and organization among the elderly produced a Clinton electoral victory in Florida. It is in the Republican Party's interest to organize Christian conservatives in the South to offset the Democratic Party's advantage among African-Americans in the region. But it is unlikely that were the nation the only base of votes that any campaign would find it cost-effective to devote any resources to organization and involvement and that, in turn, would undermine the already declining base of political participation and American pluralism.[27]

Third, according to Gans, the success of American democracy has rested, in part, on achieving a balance between the will and desires of the majority of Americans and recognizing the rights and needs of various minorities. The Electoral College, he asserted, serves to protect the latter in national politics.

"To take the most obvious example, the number of farmers in the United States has dwindled so precipitously that nationally they are no longer a serious numerical factor in electoral outcomes—despite the fact that most of the food we have on our tables is due to their individual and collective effort.

In a system of direct elections, their concerns could easily be ignored. But because their votes are critical to winning electoral votes in several mid-western and western states, their needs must be addressed, their views must be solicited, and their votes must be competed for. The needs and aspirations of America's African-American population could easily be ignored in a direct election. They comprise perhaps 12-13 percent of the eligible electorate. But in several Southern states, they account for nearly a majority of eligible citizens and they comprise a significant and, perhaps on occasions pivotal minority in several northern states. The electoral college insures, in national elections, that their views must be taken into account. Union members, Christian fundamentalists, Latinos, and rural denizens are but a few of the significant minorities whose views and needs might be ignored if campaigns were totally nationalized."[28]

Fourth, he argued, the undermining of both grassroots activity and pluralism—"mobilization and sub-party level engagement," cannot but have a negative effect on participation. "So too will the aggregation of votes solely on a national level. In most analyses of this period when over the last 36 years we have had a nearly 25 percent decline in voting nationally and nearly 30 percent outside the south—the longest and largest sustained slide in the nation's history—one of the reasons has been growing disbelief of citizens in the efficacy of their vote— whether that vote will make any difference, both in election outcome and policy result. In this age of intense polling, where the movement of national numbers in the Presidential horse-race is tracked more intensively and surely more publicly than the heartbeat and blood pressure of a patient in intensive care, it will become increasingly difficult for the citizen to see how his vote will make much difference in a national electorate in which the margins of victory are usually in the millions of votes. In a sense the existence of an Electoral College enhances both the perception and reality of electoral competition, where direct elections act in precisely the opposite direction."[29]

But of course the paramount concern according to Gans, is shifting from the fundamental principle of federalism. "Different states in different regions have important interests to which the candidate should be subjected and to which the candidates should be required to speak."[30] Though willing to adjust the current winner-take-all approach to allow minority candidates to be represented, Gans argued that *the Electoral College should never be abandoned—lest we risk our essential Constitutional distinctiveness.* For instance, there were times, particularly in the 1960s, when those who supported segregation of the races tended to use the cover of state's rights to mask their desire to keep African-Americans in their place. Civil Rights advocates called into question the structure of American federalism—the diffusion of power between the national government and the states and localities. "More recently, however," Gans argued, "there is a bi- or multi-partisan consensus that perhaps the idea of states and localities might be a good one—that the administration of many programs is better handled at levels closer to the citizenry, that the states do serve as innovators and laboratories for useful, productive and, particularly in the cases of welfare reform and crime control, better public policy solutions than the national government can formulate. In national politics, the instrumentality which forces consideration of federalism is the Electoral College, mandating the gathering of votes by states, forcing the engagement of state leaders and party organizations and concern about state and local issues. We sacrifice that, I believe, to the detriment of the welfare of American democracy."

Likewise, Walter Berns, Resident Scholar at the American Enterprise Institute, has argued for the continuing importance of the Electoral College on federal grounds. "What is undemocratic about a system of one man, one vote, and the majority rules? Admittedly, the majority rules at the state level where—except in Maine and Nebraska—the votes are aggregated, but that is where the vote of any particular minority looms larger, or carries more weight, than it is likely to do in the country as a whole. So long as a minority is not distributed evenly throughout the country, but is concentrated within particular states, it is in its interest to oppose direct popular elections; most civil rights leaders have understood this. Is there not something to be said for an electoral system that threatens to penalize a political party and its candidate for failing to respect the rights of respectable minorities? Is there not something to be said for a system that protects the interests of the states as states, which is to say, a system with an element of federalism built into it? Only twice in this century (1960 and 1976) has the candidate with an Electoral College majority failed to win a majority of the states. And is there not, then, something to be said for a system that threatens to penalize sectional candidates?"[31]

He continued, "The American idea of democracy cannot be expressed in the simple but insidious formula, the greatest good for the greatest number. What the greatest number regards as its greatest good might very well prove to be a curse to those who are not a part of that number. The American idea, which is expressed in the Declaration of Independence and embodied in various provisions of the Constitution, is that government is instituted to secure the rights of all. What is constitutionalism if not a qualification of majoritarianism?"

"The men who founded this country surely recognized the entitlements of a popular majority," Berns concluded, "but, with an eye to the qualifications or qualities required of an office, they devised institutions—the Electoral College is one of them—that modify or qualify the majority principle. Nothing could be clearer than that the Founders sought free institutions that would protect the country from what has come to be called populism. *The organizing principle of the Senate is surely not majority rule, nor are its procedures simply democratic. Federal judges are not elected at all. If legitimacy springs only from the principle of one man, one equally weighted vote, upon what meat do these our judicial Caesars feed?* Indeed, if populism is our only principle, why vote at all? Why not select all public officials by lot? That is truly democratic, because that and that only, is a system that pays no attention whatever to the qualifications of office holders. In short, what we should be disputing is the issue the Founders disputed, namely, what system is more likely to produce a President possessing the qualities required of the person who holds this office. I may be blind, or deaf, but I have yet to encounter an opponent of the Electoral College who argues that a President elected directly by the people will be a better President."[32]

According to political scientist Judith Best, if the Electoral College is threatened, the very character of the American system is at stake, "The federal principle is one of the two fundamental structural principles of our Constitution (the other being the separation of powers). The proposals to abolish the Electoral College are proposals to abolish the federal principle in Presidential elections. All of our national elective offices are based on the federal principle—they are statebased elections for we are a nation of states. Thus our national motto: E Pluribus Unum. The federal principle in Presidential elections forces Presidential candidates to build broad cross-national political coalitions. Thereby it produces Presidents who can govern because of their broad cross-national support. In politics as well as in physics there is such a thing as a critical mass. To create the critical mass necessary for a President to govern, his votes must be properly distributed. This means he must win states and win states in more than one region of the country. Under the federal Presidential election system, a successful candidate can't simply promise everything to one section of the country and neglect the others. Analogy: Why are professional football teams required to win games in order to get into the playoffs and win the Super Bowl? Why not simply select the teams that scored the most points during the regular season? Any football fan can tell you why. Such a process wouldn't produce the right winner. Teams would run up the score against their weakest opponents, and the best teams in the most competitive divisions would have the least chance to get into the playoffs. Such a system isn't the proper test of the team talent and ability. A nonfederal election is not a proper test of support for the President."[33]

James Madison argued in the *Federalist Papers* that much of the genius of a nation of liberty is its "protection of the freedoms and prerogatives of the few against the freedoms and prerogatives of the many."[34] The Constitution has succeeded precisely because federal constraints in the Electoral College have preserved the value of every American's rights, interests, and votes.

CHAPTER 13

Arguments for Modification or Abolition

"The sages have given us a practical and, as they hoped, a permanent Constitutional compact. The Constitution is still the object of our reverence, the bond of our union, our defense in danger, the source of our prosperity in peace; it shall descend, as we have received it, uncorrupted by sophistical construction, to our posterity."

ANDREW JACKSON[35]

The arguments for direct elections seem superficially clear and persuasive: Should not every citizen's vote be equal and what better way to insure that equality than direct elections? Should the nation not protect itself from the possibility of a President elected by a minority of those voting? Should our laws not recognize that a demagogue could, in third party guise, throw an election under present Constitutional rules, into the House of Representatives and thus make a mockery of the ballots cast that November?

The men and women who are asking these compelling questions and calling for either the modification or outright abolition of the Electoral College system, are articulate, well-informed, and well-intentioned. They all sound a common theme-- it is time to modernize and democratize this archaism:

"I consider the so-called Electoral College a brilliant 18th-century device that cleverly solved a cluster of 18th-century problems," Yale Law School professor Akhil Amar told the House Judiciary Committee in a hearing on Electoral College reform.[36] "As we approach the 21st century, we confront a different cluster of problems, and our constitutional machinery of Presidential selection does not look so brilliant."[37]

On that note, there have been repeated attempts to reform or even abolish the Electoral College system. More than one hundred times, the issue has been taken up by the nation's legislators or courts. Most recently in 1997, Congress debated a Constitutional amendment to replace it with a system of direct popular election.

During those hearings Becky Cain, President of The League of Women Voters, testified in order to "express the League's support for a constitutional amendment to abolish the electoral college and establish the direct election of the President and Vice President of the United States by popular vote of the American people."[38]

Cain's argument was cogent and to the point: "Political developments since the 1970s have only underscored the need for the elimination of the Electoral College system. The downward trend in voter participation, coupled with increased cynicism and skepticism amongst the public about the ability of elected leaders to provide meaningful representation are the warning signs of a potential electoral fiasco. Picture if you will a future national election in which a Presidential candidate receives a majority of the popular vote, but is denied the 270 votes necessary for election by the electoral college. This has already happened once in our nation's history, when, in 1888, Grover Cleveland out-polled Benjamin Harrison in the popular vote but lost the electoral college vote by 233 to 168. It caused a public furor then, when political office was often gained through back-room deals and closed-door maneuvering. Imagine the public outcry today, after a long primary campaign and a grueling race for the Presidency. Imagine the public's rage at being denied their candidate of choice."[39]

She continued, arguing that, "The electoral college system is fundamentally unfair to voters. In a nation where voting rights are grounded in the one person, one vote principle, the electoral college is a hopeless anachronism. The current system is unfair for two reasons. First, a citizen's individual vote has more weight if he or she lives in a state with a small population than if that citizen lives in a state with a large population. Finally, the electoral college system is flawed because the constitution does not bind Presidential electors to vote for the candidates to whom they have been pledged."[40]

Cain concluded her testimony by saying, "The time has come to take the next step to ensure a broad-based, representative democracy. Fairness argues for it. Retaining the fragile faith of American voters in our representative system demands it. We urge the House and the Senate to pass a constitutional amendment abolishing the Electoral College system and establishing the direct popular election of our President and Vice President."[41]

The most serious challenge to the Electoral College system came from the Mundt-Coudert amendment, proposed by the Republican Senator for South Dakota, Karl Mundt and the Republican Representative from New York, Frederic Coudert. The resolution proposed an Electoral College that would vote by proportional representation, which would have given rural areas as well as states with a single dominant party great advantage over the other sections of the nation. Essentially it would have awarded electoral votes by Congressional districts. A coalition of liberal and urban politicians led by the Democratic Senator from Illinois, Paul Douglas, defeated the proposed amendment by showing that the combination of proportional electors and the Mundt-Coudert provisions would have thrown almost every Presidential election in modern history into the House of Representatives.

Though the idea of amending or abolishing the Electoral College has gained a strong following in the media and among such political stalwarts as Senators Birch Bayh and Hillary Clinton, it has yet to gain momentum among the populace at large. The results of the 2000 election however, may afford the movement new momentum.

CHAPTER 14

Impact on
Third Party Efforts

*"It is natural to mean well, when only abstracted
ideas of virtue are proposed to the mind, and no
particular passion turns us aside from rectitude;
and so willing is every man to flatter himself, that
the difference between approving laws, and obeying
them is frequently forgotten."*

SAMUEL JOHNSON[42]

More than two candidates for President received electoral votes in the elections of 1789, 1792, 1796, 1800, 1808, 1824, 1832, 1836, 1856, 1860, 1872, 1892, 1912, 1924, 1948, 1968, 1972, 1976, and 1988. Third party candidates helped to determine the outcome of Presidential races in at least six of those elections as well as several others throughout the history of the nation. Yet, only in 1912, with Theodore Roosevelt and the Progressive Party, did any third party candidate poll strongly enough to even threaten to win.

Indeed, many political theorists believe that the Electoral College system makes it practically impossible for third party candidates to mount a viable challenge for the Presidency.

Media Bypass Magazine asserted that the current winner-take-all system of the College affords the two dominant parties an undue advantage, all but locking any strong third party efforts out of the final electoral process.[43] Citing the fact that Ross Perot received nearly 20 million votes in 1992 without being awarded a single Electoral College ballot, it was argued that the system ought to be abolished in order to make room for greater diversity in the federal election process.

In fact, there is a much easier way to accomplish the ultimate aim of opening up the American electoral system— simply by blunting the effect of the winner-take-all structure. This is not an inherent aspect of the Constitutional provisions for the Electoral College. It is rather the result of the evolution of legislation at the state level.

Thus, this essential reform can actually be accomplished statutorily and in the several states. Due to its partisan implications, such change would meet with great opposition throughout the 48 state legislatures who currently have winner-take-all precedents. There is little doubt that the present method of choosing electors could make it easier for third party candidates to make headway in the system if only other states would adopt what Maine and Nebraska already have in place. Thus, an essential change in the system could take place without altering the Constitution.

The present Electoral College allocates electors to each state on the basis of their apportioned Congressional representation. Each state has two electors for their two Senators and additional electors equal to the number of aportioned Representatives. Maine and Nebraska elect the two electors (or choose the electoral vote) representing the two Senators by statewide vote and elect their remaining electors by Congressional district.

This plan has many virtues: First, it would likely, although not certainly, produce an electoral tally closer to the popular vote. Second, it would certainly make each individual's vote seem more instrumental in choosing the one elector who would represent his or her Congressional district. Third, it would create an additional incentive toward grassroots activity and organizational engagement in garnering the electoral vote retail, by district, rather than wholesale, by state. Fourth, it would end the tendency of parties and campaigns to abandon states and regions where a candidate seems hopelessly behind. Fifth, it would further reduce the tendency to rely solely on televised advertising as the means to communicate and mobilize or demobilize voters. As the competitive playing field becomes smaller, the benefits of television are reduced. Sixth, it would have the effect of strengthening the parties, by allowing some candidates to run with, rather than against, their party's position on issues in states where those views might be abhorrent on a state-wide basis. Seventh, it would enhance American pluralism by making the votes of significant minorities more instrumental in the overall outcome. Eighth, it would have the important, if minor, additional benefit of making it virtually impossible for the television networks to continue their practice of declaring election results before the polls close. And finally, it would open the process up to significant third party efforts, and allow the electoral votes of third party supporters to be reflected more accurately in the national Electoral College tally.

In this way the future of federalism could be insured while simultaneously improving the current winner-take-all Electoral College system.

CHAPTER 15

The Future of Federalism

*"Those who pose as the saviors of mankind are all
too often more dangerous than the very ills they
purport to remedy. There are often simple answers to
the woes of society, just no easy ones.
Messiah always offers both.
Beware of such men."*

JOHN KNOX[44]

What do George W. Bush, Bill Clinton, Jack Kennedy, Harry Truman, Woodrow Wilson, Abraham Lincoln, and eight other American Presidents have in common? Each received less than a majority of the votes cast in the election that elevated him to the White House. *What does every elected President since 1824 have in common? None received a majority of the votes of the potential voting population and, in fact, most received less than a fourth of that possible vote!* Nevertheless, the Presidency of the United States has enjoyed wide popularity and legitimacy. Why? Simply, the government of this greatest and freest nation the world has ever known, has never aspired to or depended upon the forces of pure democracy.

Critics of the Constitutional electoral vote system find the principle of democratic legitimacy in numbers alone, and, therefore believe that the Electoral College is indefensible. The opposite is actually true , the electoral vote system is a paradigm, the very model, of American democracy. But such a principle of democratic legitimacy is inadequate precisely because it is apolitical and anti-federal. The new self-proclaimed defenders of King Numbers require a simple mandate: the majority must win and the minority must lose no matter what it is that they lose. Such a short-sighted goal is nothing less than a formula for majority tyranny—the very thing from which the Founding Fathers sought to protect us. Majority rule is NOT the principle of our Constitution. American Constitutional history requires majority rule with minority consent.

In her very helpful book, *The Choice of the People? Debating the Electoral College*, Judith Best wrote that, "Politics and mathematics are two very different disciplines. Mathematics seeks accuracy, politics seeks harmony. In mathematics an incorrect count loses all value once it is shown to be wrong. In politics even though some people are out-voted they still have value and must be respected in defeat. Efforts must be made to be considerate and even generous to those who lost the vote, to make them feel they are part of the community, for if they feel alienated they may riot in the streets. Further, mathematical questions, like those in all the sciences, deal with truth and falsehood. But politics is an art, not a science. Political questions do not deal primarily with truth and falsehood, but with good and bad. We do not ask whether a political decision on war or taxation or welfare or agricultural subsidies is true. We ask, is the policy good for the country? And, will it actually achieve its purpose? Those who confuse politics and mathematics, the head counters, operate on an unstated assumption that the will of the people is out there like some unsurveyed land, and all we need do is send out the surveyors with accurately calibrated instruments to record what is there. They also assume that our democratic republic is a ship without a specific destination. Whatever most of the people want, most of the people must get, and the minority be damned. Mathematical accuracy being their sole criterion for legitimacy, they make a great fuss about politically imposed devices, intermediary institutions like the electoral vote system with its federal principle and its winner-take-all rule. From their perspective, such majority building and structuring devices complicate their self-assigned task, distort the accuracy of their count and possibly produce the "wrong" result."[45]

According to Best, a political scientist from the State University of New York at Cortland, "If their assumptions were correct they would have a point. But their assumptions are false. Ours is a ship of state bound for a port called Liberty. On such a ship, majority rule doesn't suffice without the consent of the minority. Their assumption about the will of the people is particularly false in this vast and varied country, in a continental republic populated by a people who do not share a common religion, race, or ethnic heritage, in a commercial republic populated by people with diverse and competing economic interests. In such a country the will of the people and the will of the majority can be two very different things. Therefore, the will of the people—that one thing which all can share, which is the goal of liberty for all—must be constructed and periodically reconstructed. This requires a political, not a mathematical process. In this country, it requires a federal political process."[46]

Thus, while federalism would be ill-served by the abolition of the Electoral College, there is little doubt that some improvements might be made to the system. For instance, besides adjusting the winner-take-all system at the state level, the problem of faithless electors might also be dealt with at the federal level. There have been faithless electors at various times in the past—people who were elected to cast their ballots in the Electoral College on behalf of a Presidential candidate who cast their vote for someone else. These have generally been protest votes that had little or no bearing on the outcome of the overall Electoral College tally. But while it has never happened and may never happen, there remains the possibility of a close Electoral College vote in which one or a few electors casting ballots against the wishes of the electorate can vitiate the result in a state and nationally and undermine public faith in American democracy. A federal statute binding electors or an Amendment which would eliminate the human elector in favor of the counting of state electoral votes would eliminate that problem altogether. The essential principle of federalism would remain the foundational principle upon which American liberty stands.

If anything, the remarkable history of our nation points to the fact that radical and revolutionary actions are hardly necessary in order to protect our freedoms and preserve our ideals. From the earliest days of the Founding Fathers all the way through our national saga, the greatest reforms and the most substantial bulwarks of freedom were won not so much through dramatic innovation as through careful and conservative deliberation.

CHAPTER 16

Reluctant Revolutionaries

"The federal principle in the American Constitution
is a wholly novel theory, which may be considered as
a great discovery in modern political science."

ALEXIS DE TOCQUEVILLE

Perhaps the most notable aspect of America's revolutionary period was that its chief protagonists were not particularly revolutionary. From Samuel Adams and John Hancock to Richard Henry Lee and George Washington, from James Iredell and Patrick Henry to Samuel Chase and John Dickinson, the leaders of the American cause were profoundly conservative.[47] They were loathe to indulge in any kind of radicalism that might erupt into violence—rhetorical, political, or martial. Most of them were the faithful sons of colonial gentry. They were devoted to conventional Whig principles: the rule of law, *noblesse oblige*, unswerving honor, and the maintenance of corporate order.[48] They believed in a tranquil and settled society free of the raucous upsets and tumults of agitation, activism, and unrest.

The Founders' reticence to squabble with the crown was obvious to even the most casual observer. The colonials exhausted every recourse of law before they even thought to resort to armed resistance. For more than a decade they sent innumerable appeals, suits, and petitions to both Parliament and King George III. Even after American blood had been spilled, they refrained from impulsive insurrection.

It took more than the Boston Massacre, more than Lexington and Concord, more than Bunker Hill, and more than Falmouth to provoke the patriots into forceful secession. Even as late as the first week of July 1776, there was no solid consensus among the members of the Continental Congress that "such an extreme as full-scale revolt," as John Dickinson dubbed it, was necessary.[49]

The patriots were, at best, reluctant revolutionaries. Why then did they rebel? What could possibly have so overcome their native conservatism?

Their traditionalism—their commitment to those lasting things that transcend the ever-shifting tides of situation and circumstance—finally drove them to arms. They fought against their king and motherland in order to preserve that which king and motherland represented: constitutionalism, representative government, and the common law.

According to John Adams, in his manifesto *The Rule of Law and The Rule of Men*, it is the "duty of all men" to "protect the integrity of liberty" whenever the "laws of God," the "laws of the land," and the "laws of the common inheritance" are "profligately violated."[50] Justice demands, he argued, a defense of the gracious endowments of Providence to mankind," including "life, liberty, and property."[51] Denying this duty insures the reduction of "the whole of society" to the "bonds of servility."[52] Patrick Henry agreed, asserting that it was a "grave responsibility" which the leaders held to "God and countrymen" that compelled the peace-loving people of America to fight.[53] The combined tyranny of economic mercantilism—the politicizing of matters of commerce—and legislative despotism—the politicizing of matters of conscience—had insured that "an appeal to arms and the God of Hosts [was] all that was left" to the patriots.[54]

According to John Hancock, the Americans had been "denied representation [in either] the taxing authorities of parliament or the trade boards."[55] *In addition, their colonial charters had been "subverted or even abrogated . . .citizenship rights [according to common law] had been violated [and] their freedom of religious practice and moral witness had been curtailed."*[56] Thus, rule of the colonies had become "arbitrary and capricious;" it had become "supra-legal;" it had become "intolerable."[57] Under such circumstances "a holy duty" demanded "a holy response."[58]

The emerging consensus among American patriots—that ideological and political encroachments upon the whole of society could be ignored no longer—was confirmed in American pulpits. The very conservative colonial pastors certainly did not set out to "stir up strife or political tumult at the cost of the proclamation of the Gospel" as Charles Lane of Savannah put it.[59] On the other hand, "The Gospel naturally mitigates against lawless tyranny, in whatever form it may take," said Ebenezer Smith of Lowell.[60] Indeed, as Charles Turner of Dusbury asserted, "The Scriptures cannot be rightfully expounded without explaining them in a manner friendly to the cause of freedom."[61]

"Where the spirit of the Lord is, there is liberty" was a favorite pastoral text—as were "Ye shall know the truth and the truth shall make you free" and "Take away your exactions from my people, saith the Lord God."[62]

The churches of America were generally agreed that "Where political tyranny begins true government ends" as Samuel West of Dartmouth declared, "and the good Christian must be certain to oppose such lawless encroachments, however bland or bold.[63]

It was not the Enlightenment rhetoric of firebrands like Thomas Paine or Benjamin Rush that drove men from hearth and home to battlefield.[64] It was the certainty that God had called them to an inescapable accountability. It was the conviction that they were covenantally honor-bound to uphold the standard of impartial justice and broadcast the blessings of liberty afar.[65] It was the firm conviction that politics was not to consume the whole of their lives.[66]

In the end, the reluctant revolutionaries were forced to arms by a recognition of the fact that "resistance to tyrants is obedience to God."[67]

Thus was America's great experiment in liberty begun. And only thus can it possibly endure.

"Is life so dear," asked Patrick Henry, "or peace so sweet, as to be purchased at the price of chains and slavery? Forbid it, Almighty God! I know not what course others may take, but as for me: give me liberty or give me death."[68]

The opening refrain of the Declaration of Independence resoundingly affirms the absolute standard upon which that liberty must be established: "We hold these truths to be self-evident, that all men are created equal; that they are endowed by their Creator with certain inalienable rights; that among these are life, liberty, and the pursuit of happiness. That, to secure these rights, governments are instituted among men, deriving their just powers from the consent of the governed."[69]

Appealing to the "Supreme Judge of the World" for guidance, and relying on His "Divine Providence" for wisdom, the framers committed themselves and their posterity to the absolute standard of "the laws of nature and of nature's God."[70] A just government exists, they argued, solely and completely to "provide guards" for the "future security" of that standard.[71] Take away those guards, and liberty was simply not possible.

That is precisely why they felt compelled to so boldly declare their autonomy from the British realm. The activist government of the crown had become increasingly intrusive, burdensome, and fickle and subsequently jeopardized their inherited English liberty. The Founders merely protested the fashion and fancy of political, bureaucratic, and systemic innovation that had alienated the colonial children of the Crown.

They said that the king's government had, "erected a multitude of new offices, and sent hither swarms of officers to harass our people, and eat out their substance."[72] It had, "called together legislative bodies at places unusual, uncomfortable, and distant ... for the sole purpose of fatiguing them into compliance with the king's measures."[73] It had "refused assent to laws, the most wholesome and necessary to the public good."[74] It had, "imposed taxes without consent ... taking away our charters, abolishing our most valuable laws, and altering fundamentally the forms of our government."[75] And it had, "plundered our seas, ravaged our coasts, destroyed the lives of our people... and excited domestic insurrections amongst us."[76]

The Founders believed that no one in America could be physically or politically secure under the king, because traditional guarantees of liberty had been subverted by parliamentary and royal tyranny and obtuseness. Because certain rights had been abrogated for at least some citizens by a smothering, dominating political behemoth, all of the liberties of all the citizens were at risk because arbitrariness, relativism, and randomness had entered into the legal equation. The checks against petty partiality and blatant bias had been virtually disabled. The private sector had been swallowed up by the public.

Thus, they acted boldly to "form a more perfect union."[77] They launched a sublime experiment in liberty never before surpassed, never again matched.

Sadly, not even in our own time.

Author P.J. O'Rourke comments: "There are twenty-seven specific complaints against the British Crown set forth in the Declaration of Independence. To modern ears they still sound reasonable. They still sound reasonable in large part, because so many of them can be leveled against the present federal government of the United States."[78]

According to recent polls, a full 75% of the citizenry say that they "have little or no confidence in their government."[79] "Our national temper is sour," says Simon Schama, "our attention span limited, our fuse short."[80] We have become more than a little cynical and skeptical.

As H.L. Mencken once said: "The intelligent man, when he pays taxes, certainly does not believe that he is making a prudent and productive investment of his money; on the contrary, he feels that he is being mulcted in an excessive amount for services that, in the main, are useless to him, and that, in substantial part, are downright inimical to him. He sees them as purely predatory and useless."[81] Furthermore, "Men generally believe that they get no more from the vast and costly operations of government than they get from the money they lend to their loutish in-laws."[82]

It is little wonder then that political pundits are now warning of an imminent "second American revolution," a "civil war of values," or perhaps a whole bevy of "culture wars."

This is no time to tinker with the great instrument of our freedoms. The Electoral College is not broken. Like never before in our long and vaunted history, now is the time for us to follow in the footsteps of those reluctant revolutionaries who have gone before us. As Thomas Jefferson so aptly asserted, "An adherence to fundamental principles is the most likely way to save both time and disagreement; and a departure from them may at some time or other be drawn into precedent for dangerous innovations."[83]

Federalist No. 68

The Federalist Papers are among the most important documents in American political history. They were originally written as newspaper articles by three men, Alexander Hamilton, James Madison, and John Jay. As strong federalists, they desired to see the states ratify the new Constitution that had been drafted by a secret—and unauthorized—meeting of influential leaders in Philadelphia. This essay was written for the New York Packet on Friday, March 12, 1788 by the future Secretary of the Treasury, Hamilton. His purpose was to describe, discuss, and defend the Constitutional provision for the election of the President by means of the Electoral College.

To the People of the State of New York: The mode of appointment of the Chief Magistrate of the United States is almost the only part of the system, of any consequence, which has escaped without severe censure, or which has received the slightest mark of approbation from its opponents. The most plausible of these, who has appeared in print, has even deigned to admit that the election of the President is pretty well guarded. I venture somewhat further, and hesitate not to affirm, that if the manner of it be not perfect, it is at least excellent. It unites in an eminent degree all the advantages, the union of which was to be wished for.

It was desirable that the sense of the people should operate in the choice of the person to whom so important a trust was to be confided. This end will be answered by committing the right of making it, not to any pre-established body, but to men chosen by the people for the special purpose, and at the particular conjuncture.

It was equally desirable, that the immediate election should be made by men most capable of analyzing the qualities adapted to the station, and acting under circumstances favorable to deliberation, and to a judicious combination of all the reasons and inducements which were proper to govern their choice. A small number of persons, selected by their fellow-citizens from the general mass, will be most likely to possess the information and discernment requisite to such complicated investigations.

It was also peculiarly desirable to afford as little opportunity as possible to tumult and disorder. This evil was not least to be dreaded in the election of a magistrate, who was to have so important an agency in the administration of the government as the President of the United States. But the precautions which have been so happily concerted in the system under consideration, promise an effectual security against this mischief. The choice of several, to form an intermediate body of electors, will be much less apt to convulse the community with any extraordinary or violent movements, than the choice of one who was himself to be the final object of the public wishes. And as the electors, chosen in each State, are to assemble and vote in the State in which they are chosen, this detached and divided situation will expose them much less to heats and ferments, which might be communicated from them to the people, than if they were all to be convened at one time, in one place. Nothing was more to be desired than that every practicable obstacle should be opposed to cabal, intrigue, and corruption. These most deadly adversaries of republican government might naturally have been expected to make their approaches from more than one quarter, but chiefly from the desire in foreign powers to gain an improper ascendant in our councils. How could they better gratify this, than by raising a creature of their own to the chief magistracy of the Union? But the convention have guarded against all danger of this sort, with the most provident and judicious attention. They have not made the appointment of the President to depend on any preexisting bodies of men, who might be tampered with beforehand to prostitute their votes; but they have referred it in the first instance to an immediate act of the people of America, to be exerted in the choice of persons for the temporary and sole purpose of making the appointment. And they have excluded from eligibility to this trust, all those who from situation might be suspected of too great devotion to the President in office. No senator, representative, or other person holding a place of trust or profit under the United States, can be of the numbers of the electors. Thus without corrupting the body of the people, the immediate agents in the election will at least enter upon the task free from any sinister bias. Their transient existence, and their detached situation, already taken notice of, afford a satisfactory prospect of their continuing so, to the conclusion of it. The business of corruption, when it is to embrace so considerable a number of men, requires time as well as means. Nor would it be found easy suddenly to embark them, dispersed as they would be over thirteen States, in any combinations founded upon motives, which though they could not properly be denominated corrupt, might yet be of a nature to mislead them from their duty.

Another and no less important desideratum was, that the Executive should be independent for his continuance in office on all but the people themselves. He might otherwise be tempted to sacrifice his duty to his complaisance for those whose favor was necessary to the duration of his official consequence. This advantage will also be secured, by making his re-election to depend on a special body of representatives, deputed by the society for the single purpose of making the important choice.

All these advantages will happily combine in the plan devised by the convention; which is, that the people of each State shall choose a number of persons as electors, equal to the number of senators and representatives of such State in the national government, who shall assemble within the State, and vote for some fit person as President. Their votes, thus given, are to be transmitted to the seat of the national government, and the person who may happen to have a majority of the whole number of votes will be the President. But as a majority of the votes might not always happen to centre in one man, and as it might be unsafe to permit less than a majority to be conclusive, it is provided that, in such a contingency, the House of Representatives shall select out of the candidates who shall have the five highest number of votes, the man who in their opinion may be best qualified for the office.

The process of election affords a moral certainty, that the office of President will never fall to the lot of any man who is not in an eminent degree endowed with the requisite qualifications. Talents for low intrigue, and the little arts of popularity, may alone suffice to elevate a man to the first honors in a single State; but it will require other talents, and a different kind of merit, to establish him in the esteem and confidence of the whole Union, or of so considerable a portion of it as would be necessary to make him a successful candidate for the distinguished office of President of the United States. It will not be too strong to say, that there will be a constant probability of seeing the station filled by characters pre-eminent for ability and virtue. And this will be thought no inconsiderable recommendation of the Constitution, by those who are able to estimate the share which the executive in every government must necessarily have in its good or ill administration. Though we cannot acquiesce in the political heresy of the poet who says: "For forms of government let fools contest That which is best administered is best," yet we may safely pronounce, that the true test of a good government is its aptitude and tendency to produce a good administration.

The Vice-President is to be chosen in the same manner with the President; with this difference, that the Senate is to do, in respect to the former, what is to be done by the House of Representatives, in respect to the latter.

The appointment of an extraordinary person, as Vice-President, has been objected to as superfluous, if not mischievous. It has been alleged, that it would have been preferable to have authorized the Senate to elect out of their own body an officer answering that description. But two considerations seem to justify the ideas of the convention in this respect. One is, that to secure at all times the possibility of a definite resolution of the body, it is necessary that the President should have only a casting vote. And to take the senator of any State from his seat as senator, to place him in that of President of the Senate, would be to exchange, in regard to the State from which he came, a constant for a contingent vote. The other consideration is, that as the Vice-President may occasionally become a substitute for the President, in the supreme executive magistracy, all the reasons which recommend the mode of election prescribed for the one, apply with great if not with equal force to the manner of appointing the other. It is remarkable that in this, as in most other instances, the objection which is made would lie against the constitution of this State. We have a Lieutenant-Governor, chosen by the people at large, who presides in the Senate, and is the constitutional substitute for the Governor, in casualties similar to those which would authorize the Vice-President to exercise the authorities and discharge the duties of the President.

Constitutional Provisions

The following excerpts from the Constitution and from its sundry amendments relating to Presidential elections provide the clear standard of law, insuring smooth and [peaceable] transfers of power between some four dozen Presidential administrations across the span of more than two centuries:

ARTICLE II

SECTION 1.

The executive Power shall be vested in a President of the United States of America. He shall hold his Office during the Term of four Years, and, together with the Vice President, chosen for the same Term, be elected as follows:

Each State shall appoint, in such Manner as the Legislature thereof may direct, a Number of Electors, equal to the whole Number of Senators and Representatives to which the State may be entitled in the Congress: but no Senator or Representative, or Person holding an Office of Trust or Profit under the United States, shall be appointed an Elector.

The Congress may determine the Time of chusing the Electors, and the Day on which they shall give their Votes; which Day shall be the same throughout the United States.

Twelfth Amendment

The Electors shall meet in their respective states, and vote by ballot for President and Vice-President, one of whom, at least, shall not be an inhabitant of the same state with themselves; they shall name in their ballots the person voted for as President, and in distinct ballots the person voted for as Vice-President, and they shall make distinct lists of all persons voted for as President, and of all persons voted for as Vice-President, and of the number of votes for each, which lists they shall sign and certify, and transmit sealed to the seat of the government of the United States, directed to the President of the Senate; The President of the Senate shall, in the presence of the Senate and House of Representatives, open all the certificates and the votes shall then be counted; -- The person having greatest number of votes for President, shall be the President, if such number be a majority of the whole number of Electors appointed; and if no person have such majority, then from the persons having the highest numbers not exceeding three on the list of those voted for as President, the House of Representatives shall choose immediately, by ballot, the President. But in choosing the President, the votes shall be taken by states, the representation from each state having one vote; a quorum for this purpose shall consist of a member or members from two-thirds of the states, and a majority of all the states shall be necessary to a choice.... The person having the greatest number of votes as Vice-President, shall be the Vice-President, if such number be a majority of the whole number of Electors appointed, and if no person have a majority, then from the two highest numbers on the list, the Senate shall choose the Vice-President; a quorum for the purpose shall consist of two-thirds of the whole number of Senators, and a majority of the whole number shall be necessary to a choice. But no person constitutionally ineligible to the office of President shall be eligible to that of Vice-President to the United States.

FOURTEENTH AMENDMENT
SECTION 3.

No person shall be... elector of President and Vice President... who, having previously taken an oath, as a member of Congress, or as an officer of the United States, or as a member of any State legislature, or as an executive or judicial officer of any State, to support the Constitution of the United States, shall have engaged in insurrection or rebellion against the same, or given aid or comfort to the enemies thereof. But Congress may by a vote of two-thirds of each House, remove such disability.

FIFTEENTH AMENDMENT
SECTION 1.

The right of citizens of the United States to vote shall not be denied or abridged by the United States or by any State on account of race, color, or previous condition of servitude.

NINETEENTH AMENDMENT

The right of citizens of the United States to vote shall not be denied or abridged by the United States or by any State on account of sex.

Twentieth Amendment

Section 1.

The terms of the President and Vice President shall end at noon on the 20th day of January, and the terms of Senators and Representatives at noon on the 3d day of January, of the years in which such terms would have ended if this article had not been ratified; and the terms of their successors shall then begin.

Section 2

The Congress shall assemble at least once in every year, and such meeting shall begin at noon on the 3d day of January, unless they shall by law appoint a different day.

Section 3.

If, at the time fixed for the beginning of the term of the President, the President elect shall have died, the Vice President elect shall become President. If a President shall not have been chosen before the time fixed for the beginning of his term, or if the President elect shall have failed to qualify, then the Vice President elect shall act as President until a President shall have qualified; and the Congress may by law provide for the case wherein neither a President elect nor a Vice President elect shall have qualified, declaring who shall then act as President, or the manner in which one who is to act shall be selected, and such person shall act accordingly until a President or Vice President shall have qualified.

Section 4.

The Congress may by law provide for the case of the death of any of the persons from whom the House of Representatives may choose a President whenever the right of choice shall have devolved upon them, and for the case of the death of any of the persons from whom the Senate may choose a Vice President whenever the right of choice shall have devolved upon them.

Twenty-Second Amendment
Section I.

No person shall be elected to the office of the President more than twice, and no person who has held the office of President, or acted as President, for more than two years of a term to which some other person was elected President shall be elected to the office of the President more than once. But this Article shall not apply to any person holding the office of President when this Article was proposed by the Congress, and shall not prevent any person who may be holding the office of President, or acting as President, during the term within which this Article becomes operative from holding the office of President or acting as President during the remainder of such term.

Twenty-Third Amendment
Section I.

The District constituting the seat of Government of the United States shall appoint in such manner as the Congress may direct:

A number of electors of President and Vice President equal to the whole number of Senators and Representatives in Congress to which the District would be entitled if it were a State, but in no event more than the least populous State; they shall be in addition to those appointed by the States, but they shall be considered, for the purposes of the election of President and Vice President, to be electors appointed by a State; and they shall meet in the District and perform such duties as provided by the twelfth article of amendment.

Twenty-Fourth Amendment
Section 1.

The right of citizens of the United States to vote in any primary or other election for President or Vice President, for electors for President of Vice President, or for Senator or Representative in Congress, shall not be denied or abridged by the United States or any State by reason of failure to pay any poll tax or other tax.

Twenty-Fifth Amendment
Section 1.

In case of the removal of the President from office or of his death or resignation, the Vice President shall become President.

Section 2.

Whenever there is a vacancy in the office of the Vice President, the President shall nominate a Vice President who shall take office upon confirmation by a majority vote of both Houses of Congress.

Section 3.

Whenever the President transmits to the President pro tempore of the Senate and the Speaker of the House of Representatives his written declaration that he is unable to discharge the powers and duties of his office, and until he transmits to them a written declaration to the contrary, such powers and duties shall be discharged by the Vice President as Acting President.

SECTION 4.

Whenever the Vice President and a majority of either the principal officers of the executive departments or of such other body as Congress may by law provide, transmit to the President pro tempore of the Senate and the Speaker of the House of Representatives their written declaration that the President is unable to discharge the powers and duties of his office, the Vice President shall immediately assume the powers and duties of the office as Acting President.

Thereafter, when the President transmits to the President pro tempore of the Senate and the Speaker of the House of Representatives his written declaration that no inability exists, he shall resume the powers and duties of his office unless the Vice President and a majority of either the principal officers of the executive department or of such other body as Congress may by law provide, transmit within four days to the to the President pro tempore of the Senate and the Speaker of the House of Representatives their written declaration that the President is unable to discharge the powers and duties of his office. Thereupon Congress shall decide the issue, assembling within forty-eight hours for that purpose if not in session. If the Congress, within twenty-one days after receipt of the latter written declaration, or, if Congress is not in session, within twenty-one days after Congress is required to assemble, determines by two-thirds vote of both Houses that the President is unable to discharge the powers and duties of his office, the Vice President shall continue to discharge the same as Acting President; otherwise, the President shall resume the powers and duties of his office.

Twenty-Sixth Amendment

Section 1.

The right of citizens of the United States, who are eighteen years of age or older, to vote shall not be denied or abridged by the United States or by any State on account of age.

U.S. Code Provisions

*The following administrative enforcement provisions
of the federal law governing Presidential elections,
vacancies, and the Electoral College are contained
in the United States Code, Chapter 1 of Title 3, as
amended in 62 Statute 672:*

§ 1.   The electors of President and Vice President shall be appointed, in each State, on the Tuesday next after the first Monday in November, in every fourth year succeeding every election of a President and Vice President

FAILURE TO MAKE CHOICE ON PRESCRIBED DAY

§ 2.   Whenever any State has held an election for the purpose of choosing electors, and has failed to make a choice on the day prescribed by law, the electors may be appointed on a subsequent day in such a manner as the legislature of such State may direct.

§ 3.   The number of electors shall be equal to the number of Senators and Representatives to which the several States are by law entitled at the time when the President and Vice President to be chosen come into office; except, that where no apportionment of Representatives has been made after any enumeration, at the time of choosing electors, the number of electors shall be according to the then existing apportionment of Senators and Representatives.

§ 4. Each State may, by law, provide for the filling of any vacancies which may occur in its college of electors when such college meets to give its electoral vote.

DETERMINATION OF CONTROVERSY AS TO APPOINTMENT OF ELECTORS

§ 5. If any State shall have provided, by laws enacted prior to the day fixed for the appointment of the electors, for its final determination of any controversy or contest concerning the appointment of all or any of the electors of such State, by judicial or other methods or procedures, and such determination shall have been made at least six days before the time fixed for the meeting of the electors, such determination made pursuant to such law so existing on said day, and made at least six days prior to said time of meeting of the electors, shall be conclusive, and shall govern in the counting of the electoral votes as provided in the Constitution, and as hereinafter regulated, so far as the ascertainment of the electors appointed by such State is concerned.

§ 6. It shall be the duty of the executive of each State, as soon as practicable after the conclusion of the appointment of the electors in such State by the final ascertainment, under and in pursuance of the laws of such State providing for such ascertainment, to communicate by registered mail under the seal of the State to the Archivist of the United

States a certificate of such ascertainment of the electors appointed, setting forth the names of such electors and the canvass or other ascertainment of the electors appointed, setting forth the names of such electors and the canvass or other ascertainment under the laws of such State of the number of votes given or cast for each person for whose appointment any and all votes have been given or cast; and it shall also thereupon be the duty of the executive of each State to deliver to the electors of such State, on or before the day on which they are required by section 7 of this title to meet, six duplicate-originals of the same certificate under the seal of the State; and if there shall have been any final determination in a State in the manner provided for by law of a controversy or contest concerning the appointment of all or any of the electors of such State, it shall be the duty of the executive of such State, as soon as practicable after such determination, to communicate under the seal of the State to the Archivist of the United States a certificate of such determination in form and manner as the same shall have been made; and the certificate or certificates so received by the Archivist of the United States shall be preserved by him for one year and shall be a part of the public records of his office and shall be open to public inspection; and the Archivist of the United States at the first meeting of Congress thereafter shall transmit to the two Houses of Congress copies in full of each and every such certificate so received at the National Archives and Records Administration.

§ 7. The electors of President and Vice President of each State shall meet and give their votes on the first Monday after the second Wednesday in December next following their appointment at such place in each State as the legislature of such State shall direct.

§ 8. The electors shall vote for President and Vice President, respectively, in the manner directed by the Constitution.

§ 9. The electors shall make and sign six certificates of all the vote given by them, each of which certificates shall contain two distinct lists, one of the votes for President and the other of the votes for Vice President, and shall annex to each of the certificates one of the lists of the electors which shall have been furnished to them by direction of the executive of the State.

§ 10. The electors shall seal up the certificates so made by them, and certify upon each that the lists of all the votes of such State given for President, and of all the votes given for Vice President, are contained therein.

§ 11. The electors shall dispose of the certificates so made by them and the lists attached thereto in the following manner: *First.* They shall forthwith forward by registered mail one of the same to the President of the Senate at the seat of government. *Second.* Two of the same shall be delivered to the secretary of state of the State, one of which shall be held subject to the order of the President of the Senate, the other to be preserved by him for one year and shall be a part of the public records of his office and shall be open to public inspection. *Third.* On the day thereafter they shall forward by registered mail two of such certificates and lists to the Archivist of the United States at the seat of government, one of which shall be held subject to the order of the President of the Senate. The other shall be preserved by the Archivist of the United States for one year and shall be a part of the public records of his office and shall be open to public inspection. *Fourth*: They shall forthwith cause the other of the certificates and lists to be delivered to the judge of the district in which the electors shall have assembled.

FAILURE OF CERTIFICATES OF ELECTORS TO REACH PRESIDENT OF THE SENATE OR ARCHIVIST OF THE UNITED STATES; DEMAND ON STATE FOR CERTIFICATE

§ 12. When no certificate of vote and list mentioned in sections 9 and 11 and of this title from any State shall have been received by the President of the Senate or by the Archivist of the United States by the fourth Wednesday in December, after the meeting of the electors shall have been held, the President of the Senate or, if he be absent from the seat of government, the Archivist of the United States shall request, by the most expeditious method available, the secretary of state of the State to send up the certificate and list lodged with him by the electors of such State; and it shall be his duty upon receipt of such request immediately to transmit same by registered mail to the President of the Senate at the seat of government.

§ 13. When no certificates of votes from any State shall have been received at the seat of government on the fourth Wednesday in December, after the meeting of the electors shall have been held, the President of the Senate or, if he be absent from the seat of government, the Archivist of the United States shall send a special messenger to the district judge in whose custody one certificate of votes from that State has been lodged, and such judge shall forthwith transmit that list by the hand of such messenger to the seat of government.

§ 14. Every person who, having been appointed, pursuant to section 13 of this title, to deliver the certificates of the votes of the electors to the President of the Senate, and having accepted such appointment, shall neglect to perform the services required from him, shall forfeit the sum of $1,000.

§ 15. Congress shall be in session on the sixth day of January succeeding every meeting of the electors. The Senate and House of Representatives shall meet in the Hall of the House of Representatives at the hour of 1 o'clock in the afternoon on that day, and the President of the Senate shall be their presiding officer. Two tellers shall be previously appointed on the part of the Senate and two on the part of the House of Representatives, to whom shall be handed, as they are opened by the President of the Senate, all the certificates and papers purporting to be certificates of the electoral votes, which certificates and papers shall be opened, presented, and acted upon in the alphabetical order of the States, beginning with the letter A; and said tellers, having then read the same in the presence and hearing of the two Houses, shall make a list of the votes as they shall appear from the said certificates;

and the votes having been ascertained and counted according to the rules in this subchapter provided, the result of the same shall be delivered to the President of the Senate, who shall thereupon announce the state of the vote, which announcement shall be deemed a sufficient declaration of the persons, if any, elected President and Vice President of the United States, and, together with a list of the votes, be entered on the Journals of the two Houses. Upon such reading of any such certificate or paper, the President of the Senate shall call for objections, if any. Every objection shall be made in writing, and shall state clearly and concisely, and without argument, the ground thereof, and shall be signed by at least one Senator and one Member of the House of Representatives before the same shall be received. When all objections so made to any vote or paper from a State shall have been received and read, the Senate shall thereupon withdraw, and such objections shall be submitted to the Senate for its decision; and the Speaker of the House of Representatives shall, in like manner, submit such objections to the House of Representatives for its decision; and no electoral vote or votes from any State which shall have been regularly given by electors whose appointment has been lawfully certified to according to section 6 of this title from which but one return has been received shall be rejected, but the two Houses concurrently may reject the vote or votes when they agree that such vote or votes have not been so regularly given by electors whose appointment has been so certified. If more than one return or paper purporting to be a return from a State shall have been received by the President of the Senate, those votes, and those only, shall be counted which shall have been regularly given by the electors who are shown by the determination mentioned in section 5 of this title to have been appointed, if the determination in said section provided for shall have been made, or by such successors or substitutes, in case of a vacancy in the board of electors so ascertained, as have been appointed to fill such vacancy in the mode provided by the laws of the State; but in case there shall arise the question which of two or more of such State authorities determining what electors have been appointed, as mentioned in section 5 of this title, is the lawful tribunal of such State, the votes regularly given of those electors, and those only, of such State shall be counted whose title as electors the two Houses, acting separately, shall concurrently decide is supported by the decision of such State so authorized by its law; and in such case of more than one return or paper purporting to be a return from a State, if there shall have been no such determination of the question in the State aforesaid, then those votes, and those only, shall be counted which the two Houses shall concurrently decide were cast by lawful electors appointed in accordance with the laws of the State, unless the two Houses, acting separately, shall concurrently decide such votes not to be the lawful votes of the legally appointed electors of such State. But if the two Houses shall disagree in respect of the counting of such votes, then, and in that case, the votes of the electors whose appointment shall have been certified by the executive of the State, under the seal thereof, shall be counted. When the two Houses have voted, they shall immediately again meet, and the presiding officer shall then announce the decision of the questions submitted. No votes or papers from any other State shall be acted upon until the objections previously made to the votes or papers from any State shall have been finally disposed of.

§ 16. At such joint meeting of the two Houses seats shall be provided as follows: For the President of the Senate, the Speaker's chair; for the Speaker, immediately upon his left; the Senators, in the body of the Hall upon the right of the presiding officer; for the Representatives, in the body of the Hall not provided for the Senators; for the tellers, Secretary of the Senate, and Clerk of the house of Representatives, at the Clerk's desk; for the other officers of the two Houses, in front of the Clerk's desk and upon each side of the Speaker's platform. Such joint meeting shall not be dissolved until the count of electoral votes shall be completed and the result declared; and no recess shall be taken unless a question shall have arisen in regard to counting any such votes, or otherwise under this subchapter, in which case it shall be competent for either House, acting separately, in the manner hereinbefore provided, to direct a recess of such House not beyond the next calendar day, Sunday excepted, at the hour of 10 o'clock in the forenoon. But if the counting of the electoral votes and the declaration of the result shall not have been completed before the fifth calendar day next after such first meeting of the two Houses, no further or other recess shall be taken by either House.

§ 17. When the two Houses separate to decide upon an objection that may have been made to the counting of any electoral vote or votes from any State, or other question arising in the matter, each Senator and Representative may speak to such objection or question five minutes, and not more than once; but after such debate shall have lasted two hours it shall be the duty of the presiding

§ 18. While the two Houses shall be in meeting as provided in this chapter, the President of the Senate shall have power to preserve order; and no debate shall be allowed and no question shall be put by the presiding officer except to either House on a motion to withdraw.

§ 19. (a) (1) If, by reason of death, resignation, removal from office, inability, or failure to qualify, there is neither a President nor Vice President to discharge the powers and duties of the office of President, then the Speaker of the House of Representatives shall, upon his resignation as Speaker and as Representative in Congress, act as President.

(2) The same rule shall apply in the case of the death, resignation, removal from office, or inability of an individual acting as President under this subsection.

(b) If, at the time when under subsection (a) of this section a Speaker is to begin the discharge of the powers and duties of the office of President, there is no Speaker, or the Speaker fails to qualify as Acting President, then the President pro tempore of the Senate shall, upon his resignation as President pro tempore and as Senator, act as President.

(c) An individual acting as President under subsection (a) or subsection (b) of this section shall continue to act until the expiration of the then current Presidential term, except that

(1) if his discharge of the powers and duties of the office is founded in whole or in part on the failure of both the President-elect and the Vice-President-elect to qualify, then he shall act only until a President or Vice President qualifies; and if his discharge of the powers and duties of the office is founded in whole or in part on the inability of the President or Vice President, then he shall act only until the removal of the disability of one of such individuals.

(d) (1) If, by reason of death, resignation, removal from office, inability, or failure to qualify, there is no President pro tempore to act as President under subsection (b) of this section, then the officer of the United States who is highest on the following list, and who is not under disability to discharge the powers and duties of the office of President shall act as President: Secretary of State, Secretary of the Treasury, Secretary of Defense, Attorney General, Secretary of the

Interior, Secretary of Agriculture, Secretary of Commerce, Secretary of Labor, Secretary of Health and Human Services, Secretary of Housing and Urban Development, Secretary of Transportation, Secretary of Energy, Secretary of Education, Secretary of Veterans Affairs.

(2) An individual acting as President under this subsection shall continue so to do until the expiration of the then current Presidential term, but not after a qualified and prior-entitled individual is able to act, except that the removal of the disability of an individual higher on the list contained in paragraph (1) of this subsection or the ability to qualify on the part of an individual higher on such list shall not terminate his service.

(3) The taking of the oath of office by an individual specified in the list in paragraph (1) of this subsection shall be held to constitute his resignation from the office by virtue of the holding of which he qualifies to act as President.

(e) Subsections (a), (b), and (d) of this section shall apply only to such officers as are eligible to the office of President under the Constitution. Subsection (d) of this section shall apply only to officers appointed, by and with the advice and consent of the Senate, prior to the time of the death, resignation, removal from office, inability, or failure to qualify, of the

President pro tempore, and only to officers not under impeachment by the House of Representatives at the time the powers and duties of the office of President devolve upon them.

(f) During the period that any individual acts as President under this section, his compensation shall be at the rate then provided by law in the case of the President.

§ 20. The only evidence of a refusal to accept, or of a resignation of the office of President or Vice President, shall be an instrument in writing, declaring the same, and subscribed by the person refusing to accept or resigning, as the case may be, and delivered into the office of the Secretary of State.

§ 21. As used in this chapter the term—

(a) "State" includes the District of Columbia.

(b) "executives of each State" includes the Board of Commissioners * of the District of Columbia. The functions of the Board of Commissioners of the District of Columbia are now performed by the Mayor of the District of Columbia. (Reorganization Plan No. 3 of 1967, Section 401, 81 Stat. 948: Pub. L. 93-198, Sections 422 and 711, 87 Stat. 790, 818.)

Endnotes

[1] W. David Steadman and LaVaughn Lewis, *Our Ageless Constitution*, (Asheboro, NC: Liberty Library, 1987), p. xvi.

[2] G.K. Chesterton, *What I Saw in America* (New York: Charles Doran, 1924), p. 19.

[3] Barton James, *American Exceptionalism*, (New York: Collin Davies and Sons, 1926), p. 11.

[4] Steadman and Lewis, p. xi.

[5] Calvin Coolidge, *Wit and Wisdom* (Boston: Carnabie Publishers, 1929), p. 84.

[6] Steadman and Lewis, p. xi.

[7] Alexander Hamilton, "Federalist 68," *The Federalist Papers* (New York: Random House, 1937).

[8] *USA Today*, November 11, 2000.

[9] Birch Bayh, "Electoral College," *Encarta Encyclopedia* (Redmond, WA: Microsoft, 1999).

[10] Ibid.

[11] Hamilton, "Federalist 68."

[12] Ibid.

[13] Ibid.

[14] James, p. 124.

[15] Clarence Carson, *Basic American Government* (Wadley, AL: American Textbook Committee, 1993), p. 19.

[16] Otto Scott, *Robespierre* (Seattle, WA: Uncommon Media, 1995).

[17] Paul Jehle, "Election 2000: A Republic or a Democracy," Plymouth Rock Foundation Position Paper, November 30, 2000.

[18] James Whitson, "The Electoral College," PresidentElect.org, November, 2000.

[19] James, p. 81.

[20] Ibid. p. 97.

[21] Steadman and Lewis, p. xv.

[22] James, p. 203.

[23] Ibid.

[24] Steadman and Lewis, p. xiii.

[25] James Brennan, *Reforms and Reformers: Political Change for the 21ˢᵗ Century* (Dallas, TX: Lone Star Public Policy Institute, 2000), p. 49.

[26] James Thompson, *The Electoral College Reform Movement* (Los Angeles: Center for Democracy, 1999), p. 3.

[27] Ibid., p. 4.

[28] Ibid.

[29] Ibid., p. 5.

[30] Ibid.

[31] Ibid., p. 53.

[32] Ibid.

[33] Ibid., p. 80.

[34] James, p. 203.

[35] Steadman and Lewis, p. xv.

[36] Thompson, p. 4.

[37] Ibid.

[38] Brennan, p. 51-52.

[39] Ibid.

[40] Ibid.

[41] Ibid.

[42] James, p. 203.

[43] *Media Bypass*, March 2000.

[44] James, p. 124.

[45] Thompson, p. 81.

[46] Ibid.

[47] M.E. Bradford, *A Worthy Company* (Marlborough, NH: Plymouth Rock, 1982).

[48] Russell Kirk, *The Roots of the American Order* (Washington, DC: Regnery Gateway, 1991).

[49] Caroline Wilson, *The Founding Era* (New York: Pala Loma, 1955), p. 134.

[50] George Hewitt, *The Faith of Our Fathers* (Atlanta, GA: Heritage Covenant, 1966), p. 88.

[51] Ibid., p. 91.

[52] Ibid., p. 92.

[53] Michael Drummond, *Participatory Democracy in the Making* (New York: Carnell, 1923), p. 122.

[54] Ibid.

[55] Hewitt, p. 109.

[56] Ibid.

[57] Ibid.

[58] Ibid., p. 110

[59] Ibid., p. 34.

[60] Ibid.

[61] Ibid.

[62] Ellis Sandoz, *Political Sermons of the American Founding Era* (Indianapolis, IN: Liberty, 1991).

[63] Drummond, p. 45.

[64] Hewitt, p. 88.

[65] Ibid.

[66] Ibid., p. 92.

[67] Drummond, p. 46.

[68] Ibid.

[69] Richard D. Hefner, *A Documentary History of the United States* (New York: Mentor, 1952), p. 15.

[70] Ibid.

[71] Ibid.

[72] Ibid., p. 16.

[73] Ibid., p. 17.

[74] Ibid.

[75] Ibid.

[76] Ibid.

[77] Ibid., p. 24.

[78] P.J. O'Rourke, *Parliament of Whores* (New York: Atlantic Monthly Press, 1991), p. 9.

[79] *Forbes*, September 14, 1992.

[80] Ibid.

[81] H.L. Mencken, *A Mencken Chrestomathy* (New York: Vintage, 1982), p. 8.

[82] H.L. Mencken, *Quotations from A Curmudgeon* (New York: Legget, 1967),p. 41.

[83] Steadman and Lewis, p. 67.

The First 100 Ways

A Letter from the Desk of Howard Phillips
President, The Conservative Caucus Foundation

I*f you were President of the United States*—and wanted to put our beloved nation back on the right track—adhering strictly to our 1787 Constitution: *Where would you begin?*—How would you proceed?

The Conservative Caucus Foundation (TCCF) hopes to be able to provide answers—looking forward to the time when we will have political leaders who are committed to cutting the federal government down to constitutional size.

When FDR came to town with his Big Government "New Deal," liberals celebrated his "first 100 days."

TCCF—committed to restoring the Federal Union as understood by George Washington, Thomas Jefferson, and Andrew Jackson—rather than Woodrow Wilson, Franklin Roosevelt, and Lyndon Johnson—*is preparing, by contrast, "The First 100 Ways."*

That's the project we launched at the annual meeting of our Board of Trustees, which met in Washington, D.C.—just down the street from the White House—on January 13, 1997.

Our goal—one *way* at a time—is to prepare a "how to do it" battle plan—so that, step by step, we can spell out exactly what needs to be done by a future President of the United States—who is sincerely committed to limiting the federal government to its delegated, enumerated constitutional functions.

<u>Won't you help us chart the course</u> for "The First 100 Ways"— 100 ways to restore our government to its constitutional boundaries and biblical premises?

For too long, American Presidents have "gone along to get along"—approving ever more spending, ever higher taxes, and ever more burdensome regulations.

We say: "it's time to do more than simply focus on who's driving the train." TCCF will focus on a change of direction, moving America forward once again along the route charted by our Founding Fathers.

If we're serious about redirecting public policy, we need a detailed blueprint of <u>exactly what to do</u> when the day comes that the government is in the hands of leadership genuinely committed to uphold the Constitution of the United States—as it is written.

That is what TCCF has begun to prepare—a precise, step-by-step plan to eliminate the unconstitutional activities of the U.S. Government, while more appropriately fulfilling its legitimate functions.

I do not know when we will finally have the chance to put these policies into effect, but <u>we must be ready</u> when that day arrives.

Indeed, our readiness will hasten the day of victory. TCCF's Trustees have already authorized this "First 100 Ways" project—and assigned a separate line item in our budget to make it a success.

Now, contributions must be secured so that TCCF can cover the cost of activities approved in the budget.

<u>This is a plan for total victory</u>.

No more "preemptive concessions"—

—no more "losing as slowly as possible."

We are challenging the premises of collectivism, liberalism, socialism, humanism, and all the other "isms" which have, over the decades, eroded our biblical, constitutional heritage.

Howard Phillips

President
The Conservative Caucus Foundation

The Conservative Caucus Foundation Mission Statement

TCCF (The Conservative Caucus Research, Analysis & Education Foundation) was established in 1976.

Since then, TCCF's mission has been to provide unique, nonduplicative leadership in policy battles of strategic importance which offer the possibility of success.

TCCF publications include the monthly *Eye on Bureaucracy* and the twice monthly *Howard Phillips Issues and Strategy Bulletin*.

The FIRST 100 WAYS is an ongoing project to spell out specific steps which can constitutionally be taken by a President of the United States who is determined to end legal abortion, withdraw from the institutions of the New World Order, restore local and parental control of education, eliminate all direct federal taxation, defund the Left, end socialized medicine, and return to a system of constitutional money without a privately-controlled, monopolistic, fractional reserve banking system.

Beginning in the 1970s, TCCF has provided much of the strategic and factual guidance for leaders of key policy battles:

1) providing research and advocacy in the late 1970s in support of a global ballistic missile defense for the United States of America;

2) opposing the unconstitutional provision of federal funds to thousands of Left-wing activist groups—backing up our critique with a major fact-gathering effort, utilizing the Freedom of Information Act;

3) refusing to surrender in the battle to maintain an effective U.S. military presence at the isthmus of Panama;

4) opposing arms control treaties with America's enemies, for whom these negotiated "scraps of paper" are, in the words of Lenin, "pie crusts made to be broken;"

5) beginning in the 1970s, making the case against socialized medicine, whether advocated by Jimmy Carter, Hillary Clinton, or George Bush;

6) introducing "THE FIRST 100 WAYS" project to spell out specific steps which can and ought be taken by a President of the United States to restrict the federal government to its delegated, enumerated constitutional functions and to restore American jurisprudence to its biblical foundations; and

7) making the constitutional case for America to withdraw from the United Nations, the International Monetary Fund, the World Bank, NAFTA, the World Trade Organization, and other organizations to which Congress has unconstitutionally transferred control over the resources of the American people and the public policies which govern them.

There is much more.

In support of priorities thus determined, TCCF relies on a comprehensive range of information sources, including periodicals, newspapers, newsletters, television, radio, foreign broadcast reports, and the Internet.

To advance all of TCCF's work, support from members of the public is earnestly solicited.

THE CONSERVATIVE CAUCUS FOUNDATION
450 MAPLE AVE. E.
VIENNA, VIRGINIA 22180

(703) 938-9626

www.conservativeusa.org